HEALING IN THE NEW TESTAMENT

*Insights from Medical
and Mediterranean Anthropology*

JOHN J. PILCH

FORTRESS PRESS
MINNEAPOLIS

HEALING IN THE NEW TESTAMENT
Insights from Medical and Mediterranean Anthropology

Cover image: Giovanni Antonio Pellegrini. *Raising of the Son of the Widow of Nain.* Santa Maria del Giglio, Venice, Italy. © Art Resource. Used by permission.
Cover design: Joseph Bonyata
Book design and typesetting: Ann Delgehausen
Frontispiece: Jesus healing the mother-in-law of St. Peter. Scene from archivault, west wall, inside, Cathedral, Reims, France. © Art Resource. Used by permission.

Library of Congress Cataloging-in-Publication Data
Pilch, John J.
    Healing in the New Testament : insights from medical and Mediterranean anthropology / John J. Pilch.
        p.   cm.
    Includes bibliographical references.
    ISBN 0-8006-3178-1   (alk. paper)
    1. Healing in the Bible.   2. Bible. N.T.   Gospels—Criticism, interpretation, etc.
3. Medical anthropology.   4. Health—Religious aspects—Christianity—History of doctrines—Early church, ca.
    30-600.   I. Title.
    BS2555.6.H4P55   1999
    261.8'321'09015—dc21   99-33004
                                                                            CIP

Manufactured in the U.S.A.   AF 1-3178
04   03   02   01   00   1   2   3   4   5   6   7   8   9   10

For Jerome H. Neyrey, S.J.
Friend, colleague, inspiration;
true brother in the word;
companion on the journey
shared and continued

CONTENTS

ACKNOWLEDGMENTS

Chapter 1, first published as "BTB Readers Guide: Understanding Healing in the Social World of Early Christianity," *Biblical Theology Bulletin* 22 (1992): 26–33. Used by permission.

Chapter 2, first published as "Insights and Models from Medical Anthropology for Understanding the Healing Activity of the Historical Jesus," *Hervormde Teologiese Studies* 51 (1995): 314–37. Used by permission.

Chapter 3, first published as two articles: "Understanding Biblical Healing: Selecting the Appropriate Model," *Biblical Theology Bulletin* 18 (1988): 60–66; and "Biblical Leprosy and Body Symbolism," *Biblical Theology Bulletin* 11 (1981): 119–33. Used by permission.

Chapter 4, first published as "Healing in Mark: A Social Science Analysis," *Biblical Theology Bulletin* 15 (1985): 142–50. Used by permission.

Chapter 5, first published as two articles: "The Health Care System in Matthew: A Social Science Analysis," *Biblical Theology Bulletin* 16 (1986): 102–6; and "Reading Matthew Anthropologically: Healing in Cultural Perspective," *Listening: Journal of Religion and Culture* 24 (1989): 278–89. Used by permission.

Chapter 6, first appeared as "Sickness and Healing in Luke–Acts" in *The Social World of Luke–Acts: Models for Interpretation,* ed. Jerome H. Neyrey, 181–209. © 1991 Hendrickson Publishers. Used by permission.

All chapter art © Art Resource. Used by permission.

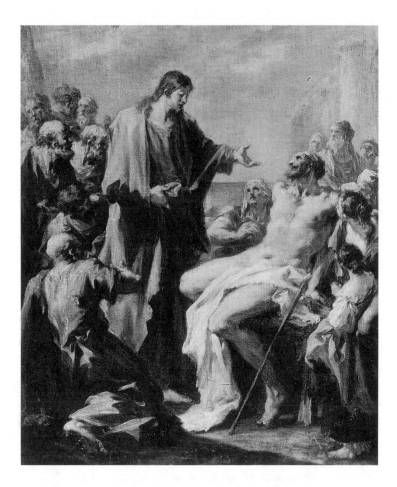

Jesus healing the lame man
Giovanni Antonio Pellegrini
Museum of Fine Arts (Szepmuveszeti Muzeum), Budapest, Hungary

INTRODUCTION

NOT LONG AFTER EARNING A PH.D. in biblical studies at Marquette University, Milwaukee, Wisconsin, I accepted a position as assistant clinical professor in the Department of Preventive Medicine at the Medical College of Wisconsin, also in Milwaukee. I held this position from 1975 to 1988. During part of that time (1974–77), I was a senior planner for the Comprehensive Health Planning Agency of Southeastern Wisconsin with responsibilities for calculating health personnel needs on the basis of demographics. In this position I wrote a successful grant application for federal funding of an Allied Health Education Coordinating Council, a consortium of educational and healthcare delivery institutions in the region concerned to avoid educating a surplus of personnel. I served as the coordinator of the council for three years. All three of these positions contributed to refocusing my exegetical training in the direction of the social sciences, notably medical, cultural, and Mediterranean anthropology.

Medical anthropology was at that time—and in many situations remains even today—something of a step-child in medical schools. Yet the multi-ethnic population of Milwaukee made it clear that if scientific Western medicine was to make an impact on the lives of these citizens, it would have to take into serious account their ethnic beliefs and practices. To his credit, the chairperson of the Department of Preventive Medicine, Sydney Shindell, M.D., LL.B., was keenly interested in making the students aware of this challenge and sought to help them learn how to meet it. I was pleased to be a small part of that department's team effort.

My task was to address with the students the role of faith in healing, the role of belief in the healing process, and in particular the significance of various healing reports in the Bible. In addition, I frequently conducted continuing education programs on these and related topics at hospitals in

Wisconsin and across the country, particularly those sponsored by religious institutions. Christian hospitals and their pastoral care departments were especially interested in learning how "to heal as Jesus heals."

The product of those research and teaching opportunities appears in chapters 3, 4, and 5. The remaining chapters build on that foundation. I have revised each of the previously published articles for this book and added new entries to the bibliographies. In the afterword to each chapter, I indicate the direction new research might take at this time on the topic of the chapter.

The same basic model of a healthcare system is applied to each of the synoptic gospels in order to discern the specific contours of each gospel. This model is based on cross-cultural research and focuses on the folk, popular, and professional sectors of the system. Such a model allows readers to appreciate their own experience of a healthcare system (for most, a Western healthcare system) and to recognize how different the healthcare systems are in non-Western cultures.

The same net, when cast in different lakes or even different parts of the same lake, may well catch different varieties of sea life. This is also true of the model of the healthcare system. Thus I repeat the model in each of the synoptic gospel chapters to determine whether there are distinctive aspects in the individual evangelist's system. It would seem there are, for while Mark and Matthew present Simon's mother-in-law as suffering from a fever, Luke presents her as apparently possessed by a demon named Fever. Because recent research on John's Gospel indicates that his community is a true anti-society and therefore different from the Synoptic communities, I modified the model for that chapter. John is less interested in healing than in highlighting Jesus' true identity.

A special Web site for this book can be found at: <www.stolaf.edu/people/kchanson/healing.html>. In addition, a section of my Web page <www.georgetown.edu/faculty/pilchj> is devoted to healing. Both sites contain links to other pertinent resources, a few of which I have indicated at appropriate places within this book.

I wish to express my gratitude to Sydney Shindell, M.D., LL.B., for appointing me to the Medical College faculty, and to Eugene Cox, M.S.W., former executive director of the Comprehensive Health Care Planning Agency in Milwaukee, for expressly hiring liberal arts trained personnel like myself. Experience had proven to him what social scientists acknowledge as fact: The best interdisciplinary research often takes place in the mind of a single researcher informed by the best of resources (Klein). Cox never failed to direct the proper resources and information to appropriate persons on staff who unfailingly produced high quality research written in a clear and engaging style.

Special appreciation belongs to my late wife, Jean Peters Pilch, and my long-time friends Dr. Bruce J. Malina and Diane Jacobs-Malina, of Omaha, Prof. Benjamin and Mary Baran, of Albuquerque, and Drs. Antonio and Marianne Gaboury of Scarsboro, Ontario. I thank them for their encouragement and unfailing support during my venture as a biblical scholar into the field of medical education and healthcare delivery. My thanks also go to Ann Delgehausen, who did a beautiful job of typesetting and finding artwork to accompany each chapter.

Finally, a tribute to Dr. K. C. Hanson, the best editor with whom I have worked in nearly four decades of publishing activity. His keen eye for detail, attention to logical, clear, and complete exposition, and incredible bibliographical knowledge in the disciplines central to my work have improved the manuscript beyond anything I might have imagined. Constructing the Web page that accompanies this book and selecting the illustrations with Ann are just two of his countless contributions that have enhanced this work. Thanks to him, publishing this book has been one of the most satisfying and fulfilling experiences of my life as an author. While his probing questions helped me sharpen and clarify my presentation, I retain sole responsibility for its contents.

Jesus healing the deaf and mute man
German manuscript, 12th century
Staatsbibliothek, Munich, Germany

1

BASIC PERSPECTIVES:
HEALING AND CURING

In October 1987, *The Milwaukee Journal* sent two reporters to six Third World countries to investigate child morbidity and mortality. Their report was published as a week-long series highlighting health problems in these countries. One reporter noted that in Nepal, diarrhea causing fatal dehydration was a leading cause of infant death. The story explained that the Nepalese seek help from the thousands of faith healers who treat the problem with a bag of bone chips and hair, "a little mumbo-jumbo," prayers to the Hindu healing goddess, Bhagavati, and instructions that parents should withhold fluids, "which is disastrously bad advice."

The other reporter, having visited Catholic Brazil, was horrified at the ignorance that allowed babies to die. Mothers don't know about IUDs, condoms, or immunization, she lamented. They find comfort in religion, believing that it is God's will that their babies die. Dead babies are known as angels, and a Brazilian proverb says that for every seven babies that die a mother gets a crown in heaven. Such complacency shocked that reporter, herself pregnant during the visit.

In summary, the reporters suggested that if "they" only knew what "we" know or did what "we" tell them, children's health in each of those countries could be dramatically improved. "We" need to spend more money in those countries making our wisdom and technology more available to "them."

Imagine how either reporter might have responded to the encounter of Jesus, the Mediterranean folk healer, with the deaf man who also had a speech impediment (Mark 7:31-37): "And taking him aside from the multitude privately, [Jesus] put his fingers into his ears, spat and touched his tongue. Then looking toward heaven, he sighed, and said to the deaf and dumb man: 'Ephatha!'"

Poked around in the deaf man's ears? How insensitive! Put spittle on his tongue? How unsanitary! Speak to someone who cannot hear? How ridiculous! Cure deafness by uttering a command? That's mumbo-jumbo!

Such interpretations—of the Third World or the gospels—illustrate ethnocentrism. This word was coined by William Graham Sumner of Yale University early in the twentieth century to describe the tendency to judge all other groups by one's own group. When people of one culture impose their interpretation of reality upon people of another culture, the result is both humorous and pitiful. To the Nepalese, the precise medical jargon of scientific Western healthcare sounds like mumbo-jumbo. (It sounds like "mumbo-jumbo" to many Americans, too!) To a Brazilian Catholic, "faith" in a mere mortal or in some pill is much more ridiculous than faith in God.

The discipline of medical anthropology developed after World War II when Western healthcare specialists met with resistance to their efforts to share the miracles of modern medicine with people in other cultures. Insights and models from this and related anthropological disciplines could have prevented the journalists mentioned above from completely misunderstanding and arrogantly misinterpreting the people of the nations they were visiting. This same information can prevent modern Western readers of the Bible from making ethnocentric judgments when reading accounts of healing in antiquity.

In this chapter, I present a model for comparing values, such as health and sickness, across cultures. Developed by Florence Kluckhohn and Fred Strodtbeck, this model has been successfully adopted in the training of health professionals (McGoldrick et al.) and business majors (Ferraro) who will certainly face the challenges of dealing with clients from cultures other than their own. It has served biblical scholars (see Pilch 1991a and 1991b) and historians of antiquity equally well (see Schultenover). Students in my Introduction to Biblical Literature course at Georgetown University spend half a semester mastering it. By the end of the course, they become quite adept. Not only can they apply it to the Bible, but they discover that the model has relevance in other courses, too, when they encounter the challenges of understanding differences between Western and other cultures.

Peter Worsley (1982) provides an excellent starting point for learning about non-Western healthcare systems. According to him, human beings worry most of all about good fortune and misfortune. Health or well-being is only one example of good fortune; sickness is but one of many misfortunes. In fact, outside the Western world, the concepts of health and sickness ordinarily include much more than bodily or physical health.

Everyone wants to know how to maintain good fortune and avoid misfortune. If misfortune should happen, everyone wants to know how to be rid of it and to regain good fortune. Worsley (1982: 330) notes that at a high level of abstraction, misfortune including illness is commonly attributed to some kind of offense against cultural values and social norms. Thus following Worsley, it would be important to know well the cultural values and social norms of a society in order to understand its concepts of illness, health, and healing.

MODEL FOR COMPARING U.S. AND ANCIENT MEDICINE

In order to generalize validly from culture to culture, all interpreters (including the newspaper journalists mentioned above) need a systematic theory of cultural variations in values and/or value orientations such as that proposed by Florence R. Kluckhohn and Fred L. Strodtbeck (1961) and applied by clinical practitioners as reported in Papajohn and Spiegel (1975) and McGoldrick et al. (1982).

In this theory, a *value orientation* is defined as a "generalized and organized conception, influencing behavior, of nature, of man's [*sic*] place in it, of man's relation to man, and of the desirable and non-desirable as they relate to human-environment and inter-human relations. . . . Like values, they vary on a continuum from the explicit to the implicit" (Papajohn and Spiegel: 20). Values determine the identification of human misfortunes like illness, the appropriate and inappropriate responses to it, as well as the expected outcomes of treatment, if, indeed, any is available.

This theory, like all theories, has three particular assumptions derived from the field experience on which it is based. The assumptions are: (1) There are only a limited number of common human problems for which all peoples in all places must find a solution. (2) Possible solutions are neither limitless nor random; there are three. (3) All solutions, including their variants and alternatives, are present in varying degrees within the total cultural structure of every society. Though one solution dominates, the other solutions are also available.

With regard to the first assumption, five common problems and their range of solutions experienced in each culture can be presented schematically, as in the table on page 4.

With regard to the second assumption, the range of solutions available to each problem in a given culture is listed to the right of the problem. With regard to the third assumption, while each culture selects one of the three

Problem	Range of Solutions		
Principal mode of human activity	Being	Being-in-becoming	Doing
Interpersonal Relationships	Collateral	Lineal	Individual
Time Orientation	Present	Past	Future
Relationships of humans to nature	Be subject to it	Live in harmony with it	Master it
View of human nature	Mixture of good and evil	Evil	Good

TABLE 1.1: Kluckhohn-Strodtbeck Model for comparing values across cultures. Pilch 1991c: 244

solutions as primary, the other two are also available as second and third choices either for different circumstances or for different subgroups within the same culture. Let us now go through this list of problems and solutions, identifying our Western (U.S.) perspective, then suggesting how Luke and his world would see the matter.

THE MODEL APPLIED TO THE UNITED STATES

Generally speaking, the solutions in the far right column represent the primary choices of mainstream or middle-class U.S. citizens.

HUMAN ACTIVITY

Mainstream Americans emphasize doing over being or being-in-becoming. This is evident in the American preference for competition, a sense of fair play, setting goals, and achieving them. This is what makes Americans tick. Being, the spontaneous expression of impulses and desires, is acceptable in some instances, such as vacations, parties, and the like, but it clearly interferes with orderly achievement. It is, therefore, a second-order value orientation in U.S. culture.

The third-order choice of value orientation, being-in-becoming, aims at activities that develop all aspects of the self as an integrated whole. Increasing numbers of U.S. citizens, though still a minority of the population, select being-in-becoming as their primary choice of value. This is confirmed by the continued growth of multitudinous and variously defined holistic groups, whether they specialize in health, spirituality, or even skiing! Being-in-becoming also describes a conviction that human beings develop through stages, a perspective that has become very popular in recent Western developmental psychology, thus offering an alternative problem-solving strategy uncommon among mainstream U.S. citizens but popular among subgroups.

HUMAN RELATIONSHIPS

Mainstream U.S. citizens are, by socialization and deliberate choice, highly individualistic. Some anthropologists note that U.S. citizens form the most highly individualistic society in recorded history (Geertz 1976: 225; he goes on to note that this way of being human is, "however incorrigible it may seem to us, a rather peculiar idea within the context of the world's cultures."). In this perspective, individual goals have primacy over the goals of either the collateral group (equals, other citizens, friends or kin) or the lineal group (superiors, leaders, the government).

TEMPORAL FOCUS OF LIFE

Mainstream U.S. citizens are definitely future oriented: The future is bigger and better, and no one wants to be considered old-fashioned by holding on to old things. Futurism is a popular enterprise, and future planning (from ten to twenty-five years hence) is essential to the success of any corporate venture. This is also seen in such things as insurance policies, long-term investments, retirement funds, and advanced education that can last past thirty years old. Often the present is not thoroughly enjoyed because the future is felt to impinge: "Only two more days till vacation ends and school or work begins again." The insignificance of the past to Americans is demonstrated by a widespread ignorance of (anybody's) history except for one's personal life span. Only the steady increase of elderly people (85 years old and older, the fastest growing age-cohort at the present time) is challenging the belief that the "youth [alone] are the future of America" and forcing people to deal with the past, however reluctantly.

RELATIONSHIPS TO NATURE

Mainstream U.S. citizens are nearly unanimously convinced that nature exists to be mastered and put at the service of humans. We bridge rivers and bays, make lakes where none existed before, blast holes through mountains and so on. Only when mastery is not possible will Americans accept being subject to nature. Health plagues like the AIDS epidemic are made tolerable by the firm conviction that sooner or later they will be mastered. Hence, being subject to nature is a second-order value orientation.

Most Americans have difficulty understanding cultures that want to live in harmony with nature (Native Americans, for example). In mainstream U.S. culture, this would be a last choice. Even where a new drug may be little more than an improved understanding of a natural resource (for example, taxol derived from the Pacific Yew tree as chemotherapy against some cancers), the ability to master nature reduces the ability to appreciate learning how to live in harmony with nature. Those who prefer that harmony are urging scientists to create a synthetic replacement for taxol lest the tree become extinct.

Assessment of Human Nature

Mainstream U.S. citizens believe that human nature is neutral but perfectible. This perception, a gift from the Enlightenment, creates the expectation that individuals will learn to control the tendencies of human nature. Yet anything that lessens willpower (control) also lessens accountability. Though violence should be controlled, inebriation or temporary insanity is considered to lessen responsibility for violent behavior. Even so, some Americans still maintain the Puritan (and early American) belief that humans are basically evil but perfectible—what Jonathan Edwards called "sinners in the hands of an angry God."

The configuration, then, of the primary value orientations peculiar to mainstream U.S. culture emphasizes:
1. doing or achieving,
2. individualism,
3. future-orientation,
4. mastery over nature,
5. a view of human nature as neutral or good.

It is not surprising that Engelhardt Jr. (1981: 32) (who holds a different definition of health) offers the following representative definition of health from this value-perspective:

[Health is] the ability to perform *(doing)* those functions which allow the organism to maintain itself *(individualism),* all other things being equal, in the range of activity *(doing)* open to most other members of the species (for example, within two standard deviations from the norm) and which are conducive toward the maintenance of the species *(human nature is neutral or good).*

Presupposed in this definition is strong faith in scientific Western medicine's current and continued mastery of nature (the ability to eradicate disease, improve upon nature with artificial limbs and organ transplants, develop wonder drugs, etc.) as well as the conviction that human beings who do get sick or disabled are of good nature and will try to regain normal function as soon a possible by seeking out the appropriate physician, dentist, or surgeon and complying with the prescribed therapy. A "malingerer" is considered to have a flawed yet perfectible nature. Such a person can be shown the error of this choice and urged to hew the culturally accepted line.

THE MODEL APPLIED TO THE NEW TESTAMENT

In the ancient Mediterranean world, we find a totally different perception of problems and solutions than in the West. First-century Palestinian society in general might be considered similar to Greek rural society, whose primary value orientation preferences tend to emphasize a blend of the perspectives under the left and middle columns of the chart above: being (spontaneity), collateral relationships, the present, subjugation to nature, and a view of human nature as a mixture of good and bad (Papajohn and Spiegel 180).

HUMAN ACTIVITY

Being as a primary value orientation is manifested in the spontaneous expression of impulses and desires. We note this in the reaction of the towns-folk in Nazareth to Jesus' statement that no prophet is without honor except in his own country: "When they heard this all in the synagogue were filled with wrath. And they rose up and put him out of the city . . ." (Luke 4:28). The proverb Jesus directed to his townsfolk was an insult, and they perceived that immediately. The refusal to act spontaneously is criticized as deviating from social expectations: "They [this generation]," said Jesus, "are like children sitting in the marketplace and calling to one another, 'we piped to you, and you did not dance; we wailed, and you did not weep' " (Luke 7:31-35//Matt. 11:16-19). Failure to respond spontaneously spoils the children's game; it shatters one's understanding of how a culture is supposed to work.

Another perspective on this value orientation of being is a certain gradation of preferences. Life is obviously preferable to death. For example, a centurion pleads for his slave who is at the point of death (Luke 7:1-10), and Jesus restores a widow's only son to life (7:11-17). Life in a good state of being (clean, pure, whole) is preferable to life in an undesirable state (unclean with leprosy, blind, deaf, mute). Hence in 5:12-16 and 17:11-19, Jesus restores lepers to a clean state of being.

The second order choice of human activity in first-century Palestine is being-in-becoming, that is, the concern for developing all aspects of the human person. The human ills reported in the Synoptics can be clustered according to the three symbolic body zones affected: heart-eyes (the zone of emotion-fused thought), mouth-ears (the zone of self-expressive speech), and hands-feet (the zone of purposeful activity) (Pilch 1985a; 1986; Malina 1993: 73–81).

The last order choice is doing, the purposeful planning of activity to achieve a goal. Perceptive readers of Luke–Acts might note that Jesus seems precisely to urge doing as a first choice. "Why do you call me 'Lord, Lord,' and not *do* what I tell you?" (Luke 6:46-49). Jesus identifies his "real" kin as "those who hear the word of God and *do* it" (Luke 8:19-21). And in response to the woman who uttered a blessing on his mother, Jesus countered with: "Rather, how honorable are those who hear the word of God and *keep* it!" (Luke 11:27-28). Yet his own prime example of doing the will of God is his rather passive prayer in the garden: "Father, if you are willing, remove this cup from me; nevertheless not my will, but yours, be done" (Luke 22:42), in which he appears to passively accept his fate in the trial and execution narratives.

These and other passages (Luke 6:43-44; 8:11-15; etc.) highlight Jesus as prophet giving spontaneous expression to his Spirit-inspired impulses and desires (being) that urge his Mediterranean listeners to re-order their values from an emphasis on being to an emphasis on doing. In this, as in many instances, Jesus is counter-structural rather than counter-cultural. His culture, after all, presented all three options but arranged them differently from the way Jesus would have them.

HUMAN RELATIONSHIPS

When collateral relationships constitute the primary value orientations, group goals are preferable to individual goals. In this kind of situation, people relate to each other on the basis of the goals of the laterally extended group. When Peter's mother-in-law is healed, Luke notes that "immediately she rose and served them" (4:38-39). The woman's cultural role was to serve at table, a group-oriented task or goal. Had she desired to run about and broadcast her good fortune, her individual purpose would have to be subordinated to the group expectation of what a dutiful woman or wife ought to do. This value preference characterizes first-century Mediterranean groups such as the Judean peasantry and the Jesus group. It also is evident in Jesus' preaching and teaching.

Another example of collateral relationships is the report: "All those who had any that were sick with various diseases brought them to Jesus" (Luke 4:40) and he healed them. The extended family brings its sick member to

Jesus for healing, demonstrating their strong lateral or horizontal relationships with kin and neighbors. Similarly, Jairus, the ruler of the synagogue, can confidently ask Jesus to heal his only daughter (Luke 8:40-42, 49-56) perhaps because he feels kin with Jesus through synagogal bonds. Jesus has already taught and healed others in the synagogue, so would he not heal the only child of a synagogue official?

Emphasis on collateral relationships or cooperation with others (rather than competition) is also revealed in passages that reflect aspects of dyadic contract as well as patron-client relationships. When Jesus occasions an unexpected, large catch of fish for Simon, James, and John, they reciprocate by leaving everything and following him (Luke 5:1-11), according to the principles of dyadic contract in which a favor received (a super-abundant catch of fish) entails a favor owed (loyalty, discipleship). Recall also what Luke said about the women who followed Jesus: "They had been healed of evil spirits and infirmities" (Luke 8:2). They reciprocate Jesus' healing with various forms of assistance out of their means. While some people who are healed repay their debt directly to Jesus by following him, Jesus himself advises the seventy of an alternative, acceptable form of reciprocity in terms of collateral relationships: "Whenever you enter a town and they receive you, eat what is set before you." As laborers, they deserve support for preaching a word of peace. And he implies that on the basis of the demands of dyadic contracts, they should reciprocate this hospitality by healing the sick in that town (Luke 10:8). Healing, then, can be an integral part of collateral relationships.

Other groups in the ancient Mediterranean world would select lineal relationships as a primary value orientation; that is, they would order their behavior primarily in terms of some hierarchical perspective or some vertical dimension. Thus Jesus' audience is startled to observe that he commands unclean spirits with authority and power, and they come out of the person they have possessed (Luke 4:36). In their perspective, this power over spirits puts Jesus in a higher social position than theirs. Similarly, the centurion whose slave is ill recognizes that Jesus' superiority over the forces of sickness and death parallels his own superior position to the soldiers under his command (Luke 7:1-10). Such a view reflects the typical primary value preference for vertical relationships in Roman society. Jesus has only to say a word and his will is accomplished (7:7-8).

A society that attends to hierarchical ordering is always interested in learning "who's in charge." In matters of health and healing, this is a fundamental concern. Jesus' enemies believe that he is subservient to Beelzebub, prince of demons, by whose power he can cast out demons (Luke 11:15). In

Acts, when Peter is asked, "By what power or name do you do this (that is, heal a lame person)?" he responds: "By the name of Jesus Messiah from Nazareth this man is standing before you well" (Acts 4:7, 10).

TEMPORAL FOCUS OF LIFE

Relative to time values, peasant societies are primarily oriented toward the present time. Peasants worry about the crop or the flock today, day to day. Hence, it is not surprising to find in the prayer Jesus recommends a petition for *daily* bread (Luke 11:3). Indeed, literally the text reads: give us today tomorrow's bread! In that world, tomorrow is part of the rather widely perceived present. The future, moreover, is unknowable and unpredictable. In response to the question, "Lord, will you at this time restore the kingdom to Israel?" Jesus answers, "It is not for you to know times or seasons which the Father has fixed by his own authority" (Acts 1:7; compare Mark 13:32). Jesus' exhortation not to worry about food, drink, or clothing—so unrealistic to Americans who plan their future in meticulous detail—is another illustration of a peasant's focus on present time (Luke 12:22-34//Matt. 6:25-34).

At the same time, focus on the present results in a concern about people's present hunger. Rather than accept the disciples' suggestion that he dismiss the crowd of five thousand and let them fend for themselves, Jesus is concerned that they be fed now (Luke 9:10-17). This large number of people could manage for themselves, but it would take time, a long time. Jesus has a better idea for the present, one that will work much more quickly and effectively.

Unlike peasants, however, other first-century Mediterranean people affirmed the past as a primary time value orientation. Elites, such as priests, certainly needed to know their pedigree. At times, even ordinary folk saw a value to the past, which could validate a claim to, and secure present membership in and benefits of, God's covenant. John the Baptizer challenged his listeners' excessive reliance on the past: "Do not begin to say to yourselves 'We have Abraham as our father'; for I tell you God is able from these stones to raise up children to Abraham" (Luke 3:8). The past legitimates important status in the present, hence people of status keep a steady eye on the past.

Jesus' preference for the needs of the present moment may also be reflected in his penchant for healing people on the Sabbath. For example: the man in synagogue with an unclean spirit (Luke 4:31-37); Simon's mother-in-law (4:48-49); the man in synagogue with withered right hand (6:6-11); the bent woman (13:10-17); and the man with dropsy (14:1-6). In this regard, he contrasts with the scribes and Pharisees' primary value orientation toward the past, namely, to "keep holy the Sabbath" (Luke 6:7). Sabbath observance is a tribute to God's resting on the Sabbath after creation, a past focus. Jesus recognizes a present need and meets it without delay (Malina 1989).

RELATIONSHIPS OF HUMAN BEINGS TO NATURE

With regard to nature it seems quite clear that first-century Palestinians felt there was little a human being could do to counteract the forces of nature. Their primary value orientation was to suffer nature, be subject to it. So, Jesus' healings and miracles stand out as exceptional events in a world where humankind had no power over nature. When Jesus casts out a demon, the crowd is genuinely amazed: "With authority and power he commands the unclean spirits, and they come out" (Luke 5:36). When Jesus calms the storm, his disciples marvel: "Who then is this, that he commands even wind and water, and they obey him?" (Luke 8:24-25).

This sense of marvel in a world where no power over nature was expected continues in Acts. For example, Peter's success in healing the lame man is attributed to the name or person of Jesus, who has demonstrated his unusual power over nature (Acts 2:11-26). When Paul manages to resist and survive the natural course of a snake bite, the people judge him to be "god" (Acts 28:6). That a human being in this culture could take command of nature or be immune to its effects is wondrous and awesome. In a similar instance, Paul and his fellow travelers are pounded by a terrible storm that mortals cannot control, but over which God was surely in charge (Acts 26:21-25).

ASSESSMENT OF HUMAN NATURE

Finally, relative to human nature, first-century Palestinian belief is reflected in Jesus' retort to the magistrate who addresses him as "Good Teacher." Jesus answers: "No one is good but God alone" (Luke 18:19). Does this imply that humankind is evil? Not at all. On the one hand, this response manifests the cultural humility expected from anyone who is paid a compliment. After all, given the pivotal belief in evil eye in this culture, a malevolent spirit might hear this compliment and do something to cause a good person like Jesus to become or do something evil (Elliott 1988, 1993, 1994). Evil is expected in this world. So the common and predictable strategy is to deny the compliment.

Jesus' statement actually reflects the first-century belief that human nature is a mixture of good and evil propensities. Each case must be judged accordingly. Notice then how Jesus continues his sentence; he rehearses the commandments that prescribe good behavior (Luke 18:20). They who have

kept them can be called good. Indeed, in the Great Sermon in Luke 6:26-
49, Jesus urges his followers to do good; and he acknowledges that good
people will be able to do good, while bad people will not (6:43-45).

From the perspective of these collective insights, a definition of health
that would match such a preference of value orientations might be patterned after that offered by the World Health Organization. Health is: "a
state of complete well-being and not merely the absence of disease or infirmity" (Callahan 1973). The emphasis in Middle Eastern culture is on a state
of being rather than on the ability to function as in Western culture. Such a
definition makes a significant difference in interpreting the healing activities
reported in the New Testament documents. Even though Jesus himself apparently urged a reorientation of human activity values that would emphasize doing more than being, the people he healed considered themselves restored to a fitting state of being rather than restored to function.

SUMMARY

Not only must modern observers and interpreters clarify their own viewpoints and articulate their own values, they must strive as well to imagine
and learn the viewpoints and values of those of another culture that they
would study. The model developed by Kluckhohn and Strodtbeck and applied in clinical practice by McGoldrick et al. (1982) and by Papajohn and
Spiegel (1975) produces a definition of health and healing much more appropriate to the first-century Mediterranean world than the definition offered by Engelhardt Jr. (1981), with its contemporary, Western, scientific
emphasis on doing, individualism, and human nature as neutral or good.

In general, then, the New Testament idea of health emphasizes:

1. being and/or becoming (that is, states), not doing (activity)
2. collateral and linear relationships, not individualism
3. present and past time orientation, not the future
4. the uncontrollable factor of nature, not its manipulation or mastery
5. human nature as both good and bad, not neutral or correctable.

This viewpoint and the values it embodies fit well with a definition of
health as a state of complete well-being rather than the restoration of individual activity or performance. Sickness and healing, then, are perceived
quite differently in this matrix than in the Western, scientific perspective.
Different values are at stake.

The sickness problems presented to Jesus in the New Testament are concerned with a state of being (blind; deaf; mute; leprosy [see chapter 3;]
death; uncontrolled hemorrhaging [Pilch 1991a]) rather than an inability to

function. What a Western reader might interpret as a loss of function, namely lameness, an ancient reader would see as a disvalued state of being. This is expressed in the Levitical code where, among those descendants of Aaron who may not offer the bread, it lists: "a man blind or lame, or one who has a mutilated face or a limb too long, or a man who has an injured foot or an injured hand" (Lev. 21:18-19). Thus, the real problem for the paralytics in the Synoptics (Mark 2:1-11 and parallels) and in John 5 is not their obvious inability to do something, but their disvalued state.

In the synoptic story of the paralytic, the disvalued state of lameness was further complicated by another disvalued state: the man was in sin (Mark 2:5). Jesus was able to improve both disvalued states. In John the disvalued state of paralysis was further complicated by the man's admission to colossal cultural failure: "Sir, I have no one to put me into the pool when the water is troubled" (John 5:7). If his kin have abandoned him, that is shameful. If he has made no friends in a culture where survival depends upon making friends, that is a worse shame. Jesus improves both disvalued states, not only by restoring him to wholeness, but also by becoming his first friend.

HEALING IN ITS CULTURAL CONTEXT

Just as health and sickness are variously defined in different cultures, appropriate therapies differ, too. In Western, scientifically-oriented cultures, therapies are aetiological, that is, they focus on the causes of diseases: germs or viruses (Engelhardt Jr., 1981: 34). Clearly such a situation requires the existence of a microscope and a host of other relatively recent inventions, technologies, and the like. The name given to this specific kind of therapy is *cure,* that is, the taking of effective control of a disordered biological and/or psychological process, usually identified as a *disease* (Kleinman 1980: 82).

In cultures that are not scientifically oriented, therapies are symptomatic, that is, aimed at alleviating or managing the symptoms. This process invariably entails creating new meaning for the sufferer. Jesus never seems concerned about causes. When his disciples ask him about the man born blind, "Rabbi, who sinned, this man or his parents?" Jesus replied that neither did, and that's not the point anyway (John 9:1-41). Even in stories of demon-possession, the demon is not the cause but rather the manifestation of the misfortune, the symptom. Jesus' exorcisms are thus symptomatic rather than aetiological therapies.

The name given to this kind of therapy is *healing,* namely "a process by which (a) disease and certain other worrisome circumstances are made into illness (a cultural construction and therefore meaningful), and (b) the sufferer gains a degree of satisfaction through the reduction, or even elimination of the psychological, sensory, and experiential oppressiveness engendered by his medical circumstances" (Kleinman 1980: 265).

Biblical leprosy (which we will examine at length in chapter 3) is a repulsive skin condition (a worrisome circumstance, perhaps a disease) made into an illness (an unclean condition forcing the afflicted person out of the community). Jesus' willingness to associate with lepers (for example, Simon the leper, Matt. 26:6) reduces the social and cultural oppressiveness of exclusion from the community. Touching them (Mark 1:40-45) reduces and perhaps eliminates the sensory oppressiveness of the condition. Leviticus makes it clear that the concern with leprosy in Israel was not contagion but pollution. It was not catching, it was soiling (Pilch 1988b). By declaring lepers clean, by raising the dead, by healing a woman's hemorrhages (Mark 6:21-43), Jesus reduces and removes the experiential oppressiveness associated with such afflictions. In all instances of healing, meaning is restored to life and the sufferer is returned to purposeful living.

READING NEW TESTAMENT HEALING STORIES IN CULTURAL CONTEXT

The modern interpreter who would like to respect Jesus as a first-century Mediterranean person who seemed to help sick people will benefit from turning to medical anthropology for assistance. Modern medical anthropologists in general offer to help Western, scientifically trained health professionals to understand and assist people of other cultures. They can render the same service to biblical scholars. In the next chapter, we will survey medical anthropology insofar as it can contribute toward interpreting the healing stories in the New Testament. In general, it is highly advisable to read anything and everything written or edited by physician-anthropologist Arthur Kleinman (1980; 1988; see the extensive bibliography in Pilch 1995) and follow up his references. The anthropologist Emiko Ohnuki-Tierney also offers a systematic and fairly comprehensive approach to healing and related questions. Both Kleinman's fieldwork on Taiwan, and Ohnuki-Tierney's fieldwork among the Ainu on the Japanese island of Sakhalin, offer comparative, cross-cultural studies and reports that are highly commendable models for biblical interpreters, whose work with ancient reports about sickness and healing faces similar cross-cultural challenges. Allan Young's article and its references will plunge the beginner more immediately and directly into the midst of things, which some might find preferable to selecting the appropriate information from Kleinman's or Ohnuki-Tierney's more sweeping views.

Because healers mediate culture, the interpreter will have to become enculturated into the Mediterranean world to properly understand and interpret ancient biblical texts. Eickelman and Gilmore offer many excellent introductory concepts and basic bibliography; Eickelman's textbook is more comprehensive, while Gilmore's is perhaps more manageable. Biblical scholars would also do well to consult frequently the *Annual Review of Anthropology.*

On the topic of healing, nursing publications are especially helpful. McGoldrick and her collaborators study families in about twenty different ethnic groups, making practical applications of the more theoretical research of Kluckhohn and Strodtbeck. McGoldrick's goal is to help nurses assist ethnically diverse clients more effectively. For biblical scholars, her work provides the key insight that Mediterranean culture would view health as a desirable state, while Western culture would view it as the restored ability function.

Against this broad background, Peter Worsley's article provides a framework for reviewing the definitions of health and healing offered by Caplan or Engelhardt Jr. in order to distinguish between the Western and non-Western elements within them. Then definitions more suitable to the biblical data (as above) can be proposed, and other interpretive strategies more respectful of biblical culture can be developed. This is the process generally followed by other biblical scholars (Hollenbach 1982; Kazmierski 1992; Neyrey 1986b) who incorporate social-scientific insights into their interpretation of biblical texts. Hemer's fine exegetical article awaits enrichment with social-scientific insights.

Some New Testament interpreters seek to shed light on biblical texts by pursuing more specific information about diseases and therapies in antiquity: What diseases were known to exist? Which cultures identified which diseases, and what kind of therapies did they know? Was there any contact between Greek and Roman medicine and Palestine? Why does the evidence in the New Testament for such contact seem so slim? These and similar questions are not the focus of medical anthropology but belong more properly to the history of medicine (see Grmek 1989). Henry Sigerist and John Scarborough are reputable and reliable historians of medicine whose many publications are not only enlightening but never fail to raise questions and research topics for anyone interested in healing in antiquity. Even so, Scarborough (11), echoing the other medical anthropologists, cautions: "very often modern terminologies superimpose themselves upon ancient definitions. For medicine as it existed among the Greeks and Romans, one of the basic problems is simply conceptualization, that is, just how close were their concepts to ours." The best resource for pursuing research along these lines is the *Society for Ancient Medicine Review*. No longer published in hard copy, the *Review* and information about the Society will be moved to the "Ancient Medicine/Medicina Antiqua" site <www.web1.ea.pvt.k12.pa.us/medant>.

CONCLUSION

Anyone interested in appropriating social-scientific insights and models in the interpretation of health, sickness, and healing issues in the Bible should find these select sources very helpful. The bibliography to this volume provides more references. The variety of methods offered by different schools of anthropology, and even differing medical anthropologists, will obviously result in different conclusions. The appropriate categories for evaluating methods and models are more useful or less useful, not right or wrong. The challenge to the biblical scholar is to select or develop a method that best suits the Mediterranean culture and the biblical evidence at hand.

AFTERWORD

The Kluckhohn-Strodtbeck model presented in this chapter is still respected as a comparative survey study that allowed researchers to make general statements about preferred value orientations in a particular cultural group. (Berry et al. [1992: 51–52] offer a fair assessment of this model and the research that developed from it.) Kluckhohn-Strodtbeck selected five groups for their study: Texan, Mormon, Hispanic, Zuni, and Navaho. Individuals were given short stories that posed a problem. The question was: Which alternative solution is the best? The study discovered that it was possible to measure *societal* or *cultural* value orientations through the use of *individual* responses. Those who expressed reservations about this study were concerned that, in some respects, the characterizations of each group appeared to border on overgeneralizations.

Such reservations are appropriate but tend to reflect the learning styles or ways of thinking peculiar to individual researchers. Sensate thinkers (using the Myers-Briggs terminology) tend to be suspicious of generalizations. Such scholars do not like the global term *Mediterranean* to describe that culture continent. They insist, rightly so, that Lebanon differs from Spain, and Italy from Morocco, even though all are circum-Mediterranean countries. Intuitive thinkers are quite comfortable with the big picture painted in broad strokes. They know the picture will sharpen as one considers details specific to an individual country in that cultural continent, and will take on additional contours as one attends to the gender of the participants in an event, their specific provenance (for example, north or south of a given country), their social status, and similar considerations. Through it all, the generalization tends to remain secure and correct, at least at a very high level of consideration. A more fundamental concern is the discomfort many biblical scholars experience with using models. Trained for the most part in literary and historical methods, they seem reluctant—even resistant—to integrating social-scientific methods and models into the analysis of texts. The objection has been repeatedly raised and rebutted (or at least responded to). The most recent, and perhaps the best and most comprehensive, response comes from John H. Elliott (1993: 87–100), who collected every objection he could find and documented his response with references to all pertinent literature that addresses the objection. To paraphrase G. K. Chesterton: It's not that models have been tried by biblical scholars and found wanting. Models have yet to be tried by many, particularly those who know in advance that models are inappropriate.

Asklepios healing a woman
Archaeological Museum, Piraeus, Greece.

2

MEDICAL ANTHROPOLOGY:
SICKNESS AND DISEASE

THE MOONSTRUCK was one category of people Jesus healed (Matt. 4:24; 17:15). Plutarch described the effects of moonlight upon human beings in this way:

> Nurses are exceedingly careful to avoid exposing young children to the moon, for, being full of moisture like green wood, they are thrown into spasms and convulsions. And we see that those who have gone asleep in the light of the moon are hardly able to rise again, like men with senses stunned or doped, for the moisture poured through them by the moon makes their bodies heavy. (*Quaestiones Convivales* 658E-F)

Some translators of the Gospels render the Greek word for moonstruck by the English word *epileptic*. This translation is an interpretation that illustrates medicocentrism (Pfifferling 1981), a species of ethnocentrism that chooses to view texts about sickness and healing from the ancient Middle East in a Western biomedical perspective. Historians of medicine are as guilty of medicocentrism as exegetes and theologians (Scarborough 1969: 11).

Medical anthropologists would identify the human experience of being moonstruck as a culture-bound syndrome, perhaps similar to *phii pob* in rural Thailand (Simons and Hughes 1985: 489) or *gila babi* in rural Malaysia (481). The sickness that results from the evil eye belongs to this same category (487; Herzfeld 1986). Since all illness is culturally constructed, a more accurate term would be *folk-conceptualized disorders,* but *culture-bound* is still commonly used. No medical anthropologist identifies such human problems as misconceptions or superstitions.

This chapter sketches a basic introduction to medical anthropology for those interested in understanding the healing activity of the historical Jesus respectfully and appropriately in its cultural context. It presents select literature, leading experts, fundamental concepts, and insights and models of particular interest to biblical specialists.

Arthur Kleinman is universally respected as one of the most knowledgeable and influential medical anthropologists—who, along with various collaborators, has shaped and contributed to the growth and development of the field. By reading just the works he has written (for example, 1988), co-written (for example, Csordas and Kleinman 1990; Hahn and Kleinman 1983), or edited (Eisenberg and Kleinman 1981), a researcher can get a view of the entire field in all its complexity.

For those interested in a broader grasp of medical anthropology, Wellin surveys the five or six decades of research leading up to 1978 and highlights the major conceptual models. The extensive bibliography in Johnson and Sargent (1990) can serve as a master list for additional references on any topic mentioned in this chapter. It can be supplemented with the resource lists in Hill (1985) and Logan and Hunt (1978).

SITUATING THE DISCIPLINE

Medical anthropology is one of five sub-disciplines of anthropology (McElroy and Townsend 1989: 13–17).

1. Physical anthropology, also called biological anthropology or human biology, is the study of the physical origins and variations of the human species. It focuses on the fossil record and on the behavior of living non-human primates. Investigation of variations compares contemporary human groups on the basis of skin color, blood type, hair form, bone structure, and stature. Sub-groups include anthropometry, or surface measurements, and biomedical anthropology (growth and nutrition, health and physique, disease).

2. Prehistoric archaeology works without benefit of documents such as those used by classical archaeology. It focuses on artifacts and other material remains, including skeletons. This sub-discipline demonstrates how health, culture, and environment are related.

3. Anthropological linguistics, also called sociolinguistics, analyzes sound systems and grammars. Its contribution to medical anthropology is the methodology called ethnobioscience or ethnosemantics that seeks to learn how participants in a given culture categorize their experience. Such research helps construct semantic illness networks (Good; Good and Good) that

highlight the culturally significant categories natives or insiders use to describe a human condition of misfortune called sickness. Technically, this is the emic perspective.

4. Cultural anthropology studies the way of life that a particular group of people follows. Foster and Anderson (1978) identify three roots of medical anthropology in the earlier work of cultural anthropology: studies of witchcraft, magic, and primitive medicine; studies of personality and mental health in diverse cultures; and, particularly after World War II, studies in international public health. Of special interest to researchers seeking to understand the healing activity of Jesus is the sub-group of *Mediterranean anthropology,* which provides knowledge about distinctive cultural values, beliefs, and behaviors that illuminate the understanding of health, sickness, and healing in the circum-Mediterranean area (Gilmore; Murdock; Gaines and Farmer; Harwood; Henderson; Henderson and Primeaux; McGoldrick et al.; Palgi; Saunders; Spiegel).

5. Medical anthropology currently is one of the most highly developed areas of anthropology, benefiting from the knowledge base already provided by other sub-disciplines. Those who seek to dissociate this discipline further from scientific Western medicine prefer to call it *Ethnomedicine* (Seymour-Smith 1986: 187; Hughes 1968), but many medical anthropologists reserve this latter term for the study of healing rituals.

One of the aims of medical anthropology is to disentangle "the closely interwoven natural-environmental, human-biological, and socio-cultural threads forming the behavioral and conceptual network of human responses to the experience of illness" (Unschuld 1988: 179). To this end, medical anthropology has developed its own methodological and topical specialties. A sample is presented in Table 2.1 (see page 22). The columns in this table should be read vertically; there is no horizontal correlation. Each column identifies a sub-field and approach in medical anthropology, under which are listed topical specialties. The research results and insights produced by each sub-field make medical anthropology a particularly rich science.

MEDICAL ANTHROPOLOGY'S CHALLENGE

Biomedicine is as much ideology as science (Kleinman 1980: 301). It is guided by Western cultural assumptions and thoroughly permeated with a particular theoretical and value orientation (Kleinman 1980: 18). Biomedical specialists tend to ignore the sick person's account of the experience and prefer to rely on laboratory tests for the "truth." This approach has no means for taking into serious account alternative therapies offered

Biomedical Studies of Adaptation	Ethnomedical Studies of Health and Healing	Social Problems and Interventions
Genetics and disease	Culture-bound syndromes	Mental health
Medical ecology	Folk therapies	Clinical anthropology
Evolution of diseases	Healing roles	Addictions
Social epidemiology	Medical pluralism	Family violence
Nutrition	Ethnopharmacology	Birthing studies
Demography	Ethnoscience	Disabilities
Paleopathology	Midwifery	Public health
Stress and disease	Shamanism	International health

TABLE 2.1: Subfields of Medical Anthropology (McElroy and Townsend 1989: 17)

by other healing systems, such as: ancient, primitive, traditional non-Western, folk, popular, modern (Kleinman 1980: 18; 28).

Medical anthropology grew out of the spread of Western medicine to other cultures, especially after World War II (van der Geest and Whyte 1988: 10). The encounter highlighted just how deeply biomedicine is afflicted with ethnocentrism and biomedical reductionism. Critics believe that this posture continues to be the conventional wisdom of that profession. One must ask why a discipline whose roots are so deeply planted in Western culture, whose major figures are almost entirely European and North American, and whose database is largely limited to the mainstream population in Western societies, regard cross-cultural research among the more than 80 percent of the world's people who inhabit non-Western societies as marginal (Kleinman 1988: xi–xii).

Kleinman's observations on biomedicine, echoed by most if not all medical anthropologists (see Worsley 1982), propose an analogous challenge for biblical studies as well. Why are cross-cultural, social-scientific approaches to studying the ancient Mediterranean world so strenuously resisted by European and North American researchers?

MEDICAL ANTHROPOLOGY'S FRESH APPROACH

Kleinman (1988) lists three ways to investigate and write about sickness and healing across cultures:

1. Borrow concepts originally intended to study other domains of human experience and use them to describe health care beliefs and practices. Thus, results from anthropological investigations of witchcraft, magic, symbol, and the like are transferred to human health questions. This is a useful method in structurally simple, kinship-based societies, particularly if they are anti-introspective. The body is a "black box," so people concentrate instead on the social and symbolic conditions of sickness.

2. Borrow concepts from medical sociology (Turner 1980). This works best in research on industrial societies, but like sociology it is not very helpful for studying pre-industrial societies (Fabrega 1971).

3. Develop an evolving conceptual system centered on the social and experiential peculiarities of sickness and healing. There are two equally important elements in healing: efficacy (see below) and meaning. Biomedicine focuses exclusively on efficacy, especially as viewed in a narrow biomedical perspective. The ordinary human person is interested in an outcome, but the most important outcome frequently is restoration of lost meaning or discovery of new meaning in life. Medical anthropology is particularly interested in meaning or the hermeneutic dimension of healing.

Medical anthropology has elected this last method as the most appropriate for its interests. Its practitioners prefer to develop and advance its own ethnomedical paradigm as an alternative to the biomedical paradigm. This science needs an autonomous theoretical frame that is more suitable than any other for describing and interpreting the human experience of health, sickness, and healing (Kleinman 1980: 377).

IMPORTANCE OF MEDICAL ANTHROPOLOGY

The following comment from Simons and Hughes (1985: 29) on the study of culture-bound syndromes should encourage the researcher, who has devoted a career to studying the healing activity of Jesus, to look to other, supplementary methodologies:

> The approach advocated here is problem centered rather than discipline centered. Too often discipline-centered approaches have included subtle and sometimes not so subtle attempts to restrict relevance to Those in which I am Certified Expert (or, more charitably, to Those I am Competent to Discuss). In reality, relevant data may lie within many disciplines. And these data can seldom be organized hierarchically. Every set of human behaviors exists in a complex matrix of biological, social, psychological,

and cultural facts which shape each other. How any portion of this set of facts shapes specific aspects of behavior or experience is a matter which must be discovered empirically, and an accurate analogy is not a layer cake but a marble cake.

Interdisciplinary specialists point out that the best interdisciplinary co-operation is often that carried out in the mind of a single researcher, an expert in one field who borrows eclectically from other disciplines and creatively integrates a variety of insights.

SOME BASIC TERMS AND DEFINITIONS

Kleinman's definitions (1980; Kleinman et al. 1978) are generally and widely shared in medical anthropology (Caplan et al. 1981; Cassell 1976; Eisenberg 1977; Engelhardt Jr. 1981, 1986; Fitzpatrick 1984; Landy 1977; Ohnuki-Tierney 1981, 1984) even if sometimes modified (Young 1982).

Health is very difficult to define. It is never clear what is lost when one has lost good health. In general, any definition of health is a descriptive and often culturally normative concept that plays a defining role in a given society.

In the United States, where a major cultural value is achievement and self-sufficiency, health might be defined as "the ability to perform those functions which allow the organism to maintain itself, all other things being equal, in the range of activity open to most other members of the species (for example, within two standard deviations from the norm) and which are conducive toward the maintenance of its species" (Engelhardt Jr. 1981: 32).

The classic definition offered by the World Health Organization, "state of complete physical, mental, and social well-being and not merely the absence of disease and infirmity," is routinely challenged by Western specialists because of its focus on health as a "state." Non-Western populations, however, find the definition very meaningful since their cultural values place a high priority on well-being from a variety of perspectives.

Thus, from a general, medical anthropological perspective, health is best understood as a condition of well-being as understood by a given culture.

Sickness is a blanket term used to label real human experiences of disease and/or illness. This is the proper domain of medical anthropology, though special attention is paid mainly to illness (Twaddle 1981).

Disease is not a reality but rather an explanatory concept that describes abnormalities in the structure and/or function of human organs and organ systems. This includes pathological states even if they are not culturally recognized (Foster 1976). Disease is the arena of biomedicine and the biomedical model (Kleinman 1980; Grmek 1989; Lipowski 1969).

The concept of disease attempts to correlate constellations of signs and symptoms for the purpose of explanation, prediction, and control (Engelhardt Jr. 1981: 39). The biomedical jargon for these strategies is diagnoses, prognosis, and therapy, and these concepts lead into the field of power and politics (Glick 1967; Pilch 1991a; 1992a and b).

Illness, too, is not a reality but an explanatory concept that describes the human perception, experience, and interpretation of certain socially disvalued states including but not limited to disease (see Worsley 1982, 327). Illness is both a personal and social reality and therefore in large part a cultural construct (Kleinman 1974b; Lewis 1981). Culture dictates what to perceive, value, and express, and then how to live with illness (Kleinman 1980: 417–18; Ohnuki-Tierney 1981, 1984; Weidman 1988; Kaplan 1983).

Curing is the anticipated outcome relative to *disease,* that is, the attempt to take effective control of disordered biological and/or psychological processes.

Healing is directed toward illness, that is, the attempt to provide personal and social meaning for the life problems created by sickness. Treatment, of course, can be concerned with one or the other aspect of a human problem (disease or illness), and either or both can be successfully treated. The complaint against modern biomedicine is that it is concerned only with curing the disease while the patient is searching for healing the illness. This dichotomy separates what nearly all human societies view as essential in healing, that is, some combination of symptom reduction along with other behavior or physical transformation that reflects that society's understanding of health and the provision of new or renewed meaning in life for the sick person (Etkin 1988: 300).

Healing is an elemental social function and experience. It is equally as basic and fundamental as the gift or the exchange relationship. Healing is one of the primary forms of symbolic action (Kleinman 1974a: 210).

These definitions and their implications offer researchers of the historical Jesus a fresh perspective on sickness and healing in the first-century, eastern Mediterranean world and a welcome rescue from the tyranny of Western biomedical perspectives.

THE HEALTH CARE SYSTEM

In every society, the health care system (Mackintosh 1978) is created by a collective view and shared pattern of usage that operates at a local level and

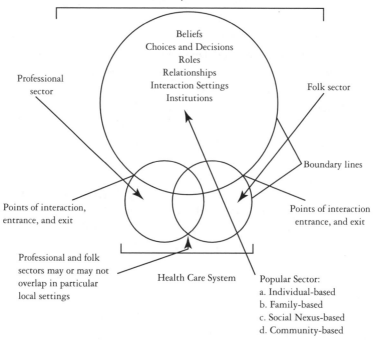

FIGURE 2.1: The Health Care System (after Kleinman 1980: 50; Pilch 1985: 144)

is seen and used somewhat differently by different social groups and individuals (Kleinman 1980: 39). Thus the health care system is a concept, and not an entity. It is a conceptual model held by the researcher. Kleinman constructed a structural model of a health care system (see Figure 2.1) that he suggested could be used to analyze the system in any society or culture (Pilch 1985: 144).

Because the whole system heals, not just the healer (Kleinman 1980: 72), the investigator needs to conduct both a micro- and a macro-analysis to see how small-scale events within the healing system in its three sectors might relate to large-scale social structure and processes.

Consider the element of power. Glick (1967) proposed that knowing a culture's chief source(s) of power, whether political, social, mythological, religious, technological, etc., will allow the researcher to deduce the beliefs about the causes of illness and how to treat illness. Social reality determines what the power is: witchcraft, exorcism, fortune-telling, surgery, psychotherapy, and symbolic reality determines the pathways by which the application of power may be effective (see symbolic healing below). In turn, political, political-economic, and cultural power determines which view prevails and which outcomes are acceptable.

Finally, Kleinman cautions that health care systems are nearly impossible to understand once they are removed from their cultural contexts (1980: 415)—all the more reason for seeking to discover as much about cultural beliefs, values, and behaviors as possible.

FIVE MAJOR FUNCTIONS
OF HEALTH CARE SYSTEMS

Five elements working together in a given system construct and define both health and illness (Kleinman 1978: 416–71). These elements are also called the *core clinical functions.* In this phrase the word *clinical* represents general health care.

1. Cultural Hierarchies of Health Values

Societies construct a hierarchy of health values, and "in small scale, pre-literate societies, as well as in many historical cultures, the fit between health values (needs, expectations, choices and evaluations) and healing (therapeutic approaches and outcomes) can often be very tight" (Kleinman 1978: 417). This is so because the individual internalizes these health values during the socialization process.

The semantic illness networks (see Good and Good 1981) of given societies tend to cluster a variety of values, concepts, and experience. The West seems to prefer metaphors of war: germs invade, the threatened person fights infection, biomedical researchers wage war against viruses, etc. On the other hand, the Taiwanese, among whom Kleinman has conducted extensive research, talk about being hit by ghosts, either purposefully or inadvertently, and thereby becoming ill.

In the Mediterranean cultural world, one must attend to the core values of honor and shame, gender-based division of society, client and patron, sheep and goats (Pilch 1992a and b; Murdock 1980), belief in spirits (Saler 1977), attitudes toward pain (Zborowski 1969; Zola 1966), and many other concepts and values that comprise that distinctive cultural hierarchy of health values.

2. Experience of Illness

Culture dictates what to perceive, value, express, and how to live with illness. Culture also plays a significant role in symptom formation (Pilch 1988b), as well as the various psychophysiological processes in and reactions to illness. Culture's greatest contribution is the meaning given to the illness experience.

This is also the first stage of healing, because the experience can be acknowledged and recognized as something specific that charts the initial path toward an appropriate response.

3. Cognitive Response: Ordering Illness
By Means of Labeling, Classifying, and Explaining

Culture establishes general criteria to guide the therapeutic process and to evaluate the outcomes. This involves creating structures of relevance: Is this experience major or minor? Important or negligible? The response involves knowing the hierarchies of resort: family, friends, the village, the herbalist, the prophet, the professional, etc. (Pilisuk and Parks 1986; Romanucci-Ross 1969).

Mary Douglas (1970) has convincingly demonstrated that illness and its consequences are intensely social and communal events. They are disruptive and often threaten the most essential values, behavioral norms, and conceptions of order. What is required is restoration of order by placing the threat in its proper framework, controlling the disruptive effect on the sick person and that person's network, and making the entire experience personally and socially meaningful.

To explore this dimension further, one needs to investigate explanatory models (see below) that differ from sick person to sick person, and also between the sick person and the therapist. The cognitive response to misfortune or sickness forms the core of symbolic healing (see below).

4. Healing Activities

In fact, healing goes on throughout the entire system and in each of these five functions, so one must consider individual healing practices within the *total* context of the system and indeed of society. In other words, healing entails much more than demonstrable empirical efficacy, important as this may be when or whether it actually occurs (Frank 1974).

Strategies include healing and preventive activities per se, which range from empirical remedies (see van der Geest and Whyte 1988) and technological interventions to symbolic therapies like the placebo (Moerman 1983; see also Dow 1986).

5. Potential Outcomes: Managing Cure or Treatment Failure,
Recurrence or Chronic Illness, Permanent Impairment, and Death

Anthropologists note that much of traditional health care is dedicated to preparing for death and making the experience of dying meaningful. It is especially at this point that health care often overlaps with religion and other cultural systems. In the entire process, of course, constructing a meaningful life is equally important. In this stage, human efforts are focused on answering the question: Now what?

These five functions provide a fairly comprehensive basis for understanding healing and health care in any given culture and allow for more appropriate cross-cultural comparisons. All attempts to understand illness and treatment can be thought of as explanatory models.

EXPLANATORY MODELS (EMs)

EMs are more or less formally structured and coherent accounts of reality, in this case, the reality of illness and its treatment. They may be and often are ambiguous and changing and may even contain contradictions and varying degrees of logical development. Social scientists note that all people have multiple belief systems to which they turn when they need help.

EMs are the notions about an episode of sickness and its treatment that are employed by everyone involved in the process (the sick person, family, friends, village, healers). These models are embedded in the larger cognitive systems that in turn are anchored in particular cultural and structural arrangements—that is, the health care system sectors and sub-sectors. Of great import to the medical anthropologist is not only grasping and understanding the EMs but also observing the interaction (see below) between sick persons and healers. This interaction is a central component of health care, and one learns about it by exploring and recording the EMs involved.

Structurally, there are five questions that EMs seek to explain relative to each illness episode (Kleinman 1980: 105):
1. etiology, that is, origins and causes
2. time and onset of symptoms
3. pathophysiology
4. course of sickness, including the degree of severity and the type of sick role (acute, chronic, impaired, etc.)
5. treatment.

The healer's EM seeks to answer all five questions. The family and sick individual EMs usually answer only salient questions. In contrast to professional EMs, those of the layperson ordinarily disclose the significance of a given health problem for the patient and the family, along with their treatment goals. A review of all the information gathered by the EMs of everyone involved in a given illness episode helps an investigator to realize that efficacy always involves both symptom reduction and restoration of meaning to life.

In practically all of his publications, Kleinman concludes with suggestions for avenues of future research. Here, adapted for biblical specialists, is his list for additional research topics relative to EMs:

♦ a systematic and holistic study of the local health care system in first-century Palestine, emphasizing interaction between different sectors (professional, lay, folk; public and private; male and female; patron-broker-client; etc.) and the relation of health care functions to their component elements

♦ a focus on cognitive and communicative aspects of the healer–client relationships, stressing comparisons of, and interactions between, EMs in the popular, folk, clinical and scientific domains

♦ a cross-cultural comparison of psychosocial and psychophysiological aspects of the illness experience in first-century Palestine, emphasizing mechanisms by which culture molds behavior and biology (for example, swaddling socializes an infant to control very early in life; loss of control is permitted in possession or in angry rage, after which the person is puzzled and repentant about the uncontrolled behavior just experienced; etc.)

♦ the relationship between meaning (subjective and social) and effectiveness in traditional and modern health care

♦ a study of local medical systems as adaptive responses to specific stress factors in the physical and social environments (for example: fathers use physical punishment in rearing sons [Pilch 1993]; a son who becomes a violent adult explains violent behavior through possession by a violent spirit; the violence is tamed by casting out the demon).

TRANSACTION: THE INTERACTION WITH THE HEALER

While it is the whole system and not just the healer that heals, the transactions between sick people and healers are critical (Mason et al. 1969). All transactions between the sick person and the healer(s) should be considered fundamentally hermeneutic (Good and Good 1981; Pilch 1988b). What takes place in the interaction is interpretation of symbols and signs in terms of very particular interpretive schemata.

The diverse EMs that all the actors in a healing transaction bring to the event influence the interactions and interpretations that take place. The sick person and the healer are best understood as engaging in the interpretation of the context of the encounter, which itself is symbolic, and of the symbolic forms that are manipulated by the other during the encounter. Symbols include words, acts, events, and gestures. The healing encounter is recognized as a distinctive kind of encounter, and the specific encounter under consideration is either a new form of interaction or a repetition of a previously known form of encounter. What the encounter produces is *understanding* rather than new knowledge or explanation (Gaines 1982: 244).

In a recent reflection on these encounters, Kleinman (1988: 115–16) constructed another model for comparing healing systems across cultures. The following summary of its key points omits the detail that is understandably required by Kleinman's interest in contemporary industrialized cultures where biomedical systems prevail, as well as the traditional cultures he studies in the Far East.

1. Setting: folk, popular, professional
2. Characteristics of the interaction:
   a. Number of participants
   b. Time character: episodic or continuous, brief or lengthy
   c. Quality of relationship: formal or informal, authoritarian or dyadic, etc.
3. Characteristics of the healer:
   a. Personality
   b. Training
   c. Type of practice
   d. Insight into the process
4. Idioms of communication:
   a. Mode: somatic, religious, moral, social, etc.
   b. Code: nonverbal, verbal, special semiotic system
   c. EM of a particular illness episode—for example, shared, conflicting, open, tacit, etc.
   d. Rhetorical devices for narratizing illness and negotiating treatment
   e. Interpretation.
5. Clinical reality: sacred or secular, disease-oriented or illness-oriented, focus of treatment (sick person, family, etc.), symbolic and/or instrumental interventions, etc.
6. Therapeutic stages and mechanisms: process, mechanisms of change (catharsis, confession, altered state of consciousness, etc.)
7. Extratherapeutic aspects: social control, political implications, etc.

Kleinman designed the model specifically for examining symbolic healing systems (for example, forms of religious healing, shamanism, various lay psychotherapies sometimes called ministries). With appropriate modifications and fine-tuning, which is standard procedure in the construction and application of models, it can serve well for analyzing healing interactions in the first-century world.

SYMBOLIC HEALING

Medical anthropologists generally agree that religious healing, shamanism, and Western psychotherapy are versions of one and the same thing: symbolic healing (Dow 1986: 56; Moerman 1983; Kleinman 1988: 131). In symbolic healing, the therapist or healer mediates culture. What is especially important is the metaphorical structure of that culture. This is as decisive in effectiveness as any other elements, whether physiological, pharmacological, or anything else. Symbolic healing is best understood by examining the four essential structural processes involved in accomplishing it.

Stage 1. Symbolic Bridge. It is important to establish a symbolic bridge between personal experience, social relations, and cultural meanings. Every system of symbolic healing is based on a model of experiential reality that is called the mythic world. If this world does not derive from society's shared meaning, then it derives from initiation into a particular system of healing such as a psychoanalytic relationship or a charismatic prayer group.

The particular cultural mythic world contains knowledge that is true experientially but not necessarily empirically. Together, the healer and the sick person agree to particularize a segment of the cultural mythic world for use in a particular case of symbolic healing (Dow 1986: 61).

The mythic world contains the symbols that link the social system to the self system of the sick person. The relationship of these two systems to other systems can be seen in Dow's hierarchy of living systems presented in Table 2.2. A symbolic bridge between two systems will occur at different points in different cultures.

Environment	System	Units
Natural environment	Ecological	Populations
Social environment	Social	Individuals
Individual environment	Self	Somatic systems
Body	Somatic	Cells, etc.
Cells	Molecular	Molecules (genes)

TABLE 2.2: Hierarchy of Living Systems (Dow 1986: 62)

The hierarchy of linked systems in this table is the biopsychocultural basis for healing. For instance, the individual experience (serious loss) is linked with a group's master symbols (Easter; crucified Christ), which in turn express the deep cultural grammar governing how an individual orients self to others and to the inner world. The cultural grammar is found in the central myths (Scripture). Both Dow and Kleinman suggest the associations noted in parentheses that have preceded. Just as illness is expressed at different levels of this hierarchy, so is healing a transformation of these linked systems at various or all levels.

Stage 2. Relating the Sick Person to the Mythic World. A healer activates the symbolic connections for a sick person. The healer persuades the sick person that the problem can be related to some part of the mythic world. For instance, Peter's mother-in-law in the Lukan account suffers from a demon named Fever and therefore she can be treated by exorcism (Pilch 1991a; 1992b). In small-scale pre-industrial societies, the healer, the sick person, and the family usually agree about these core meanings.

Stage 3. Transactional Symbols. A healer employs mediating (also called *transactional*) symbols that are particularized from the general meaning system, and guides therapeutic change in the sick person's emotional reactions. The focus on emotion in the self system works by way of hierarchical linkage in the somatic system.

It is not just the healer's rhetorical skill at work here. Rather, the participants in symbolic healing share mutual expectations that shape and name the clinical reality, that is, the illness. Then the healer generalizes the personal experience into the therapeutic meaning system, and the sick person particularizes that symbolic meaning into personal experience. One illustration of such a transactional symbol is the sand paintings of Navaho spirits as used with other techniques by Navaho healers.

Stage 4. Confirmation. The healer confirms the transformation of the particularized symbolic meaning. Thus, an intrusive spirit, now named, is subjected to specific rituals of exorcism. "In anthropological terms, the healing interaction fosters this transformation as a work of culture: the making over of psychophysiological process into meaningful experience and the affirmation of success" (Kleinman 1988: 134).

Most symbolic healing around the planet takes place in the popular sector, that is the family and community, and the folk sector, that is the non-professional, non-bureaucratic, specialist sector especially in societies that lack professionalization. These are ordinary folk considered to be specially gifted to heal (Kleinman 1988: 117). Most healing is not long-term, divorced from everyday life encounters between participants, psychologically minded, secular, or oriented to the needs and rights of the individual vis-à-vis those of the family and community. The therapeutic relationship is authoritarian in nearly all cultures except the West. This is what one would expect in the sociocentric or collectivistic non-Western cultures as contrasted with egocentric or individualistic Western culture.

Clearly, interpretation is the core task of healing cross-culturally (Kleinman 1988: 119). Non-Western healing systems (Worsley 1982) ordinarily emphasize sacred reality, illness orientation (that is, they take the sick person's account to be the real problem), symbolic intervention, interrogative structure, sociocentric but particularly family-centered locus of control, and substantial expectations of change and even cure (in the technical sense defined in this chapter).

EFFICACY

Do (did) real cures really happen? Do these techniques and strategies really work? Such questions routinely emerge from Western skeptics who are un-aware that they stem from the biomedical reductionism into which natives of Western culture have been socialized for almost a century now. Efficacy is "the perceived capacity of a given practice to affect sickness in some desirable way" (Young 1982, 277). Actually, efficacy can mean any number of things ranging from total symptom reduction to some physical sign, like fever, vomiting, or the like, which can be interpreted as a required proximate effect indicating that the ultimate anticipated outcome is on the way (Etkin 1988, 301–2). From the perspective of medical anthropology, curing is efficacious when biomedical changes take place; healing is efficacious when the people who seek it say it is.

What is crucial to evaluating efficacy is understanding the cultural expectation and the biological outcomes at various stages of the therapeutic processes. Efficacy is always a cultural construct (Kleinman 1974a: 210).

The healing dialectic has been considered effective when the bonds between the sick individual and the group, weakened by disease, are strengthened, social values reaffirmed, and the notion of social order no longer threatened by illness and death. Healing is also effective when the individual experience of illness has been made meaningful, personal suffering shared, and the individual leaves the marginal situation of sickness and is reincorporated—in health or even death—back into the social body.

Medical anthropologists cannot totally explain how cultural factors are related to the healing process. There is more here than meets the biomedical eye. The best contemporary hypothesis is that the sick person in a specific context uses the semantic and symbolic resources available and creates meaning. The meaning may be wholesome *(placebo)* or noxious *(nocebo)*.

Moerman (1983) records the traditional wisdom on this point: "meaning mends" and "metaphor can heal." Medical anthropologists note that placebos mend when they are not understood to be that. Metaphors heal best when they are taken literally and their symbolic identity is not recognized. When they are demystified, they tend to lose their effectiveness.

In other words, healing boils down to meaning and the transformation of experience. The change or transformation is created by all participants who effectively enact culturally authorized interpretations. When demons are exorcised, the anxious client believes the cause of the problem is gone. This conviction is affirmed by the healer and encouraged by the social circle. It alters the client's cognitive processes from apprehension to calm.

What has changed? The life problems may or may not still be present, but their perception is no longer the same. "Altered meanings exert practical efficacy in the felt experience of the patient" (Kleinman 1988: 134).

CONCLUSION

Medical anthropologists believe that one advantage of ethnomedical and cross-cultural research is that it forces biomedical practitioners out of a narrow professional orientation and exposes them to aspects of human health that are frequently hidden by the role and social space the practitioners exercise in modern Western culture. Medical anthropology could work the same effect for the similarly specialized biblical researcher.

In traditional cultures it is not always possible to separate medicine from the religious system as is routinely done in the West. Religion can be viewed as a cultural adaptive response to a much wider range of suffering and misfortune, of which human sickness is only a small part. For this reason, Kleinman (1973: 57) insists that "without first possessing a fairly deep understanding of its cultural setting, it would seem impossible to understand a given system of medicine; this seems to hold as well for systems of scientific knowledge." The biblical researcher would thus move from a study of medical anthropology to the equally important study of Mediterranean anthropology. There is no other way to learn the concepts and values that govern and shape the understanding of healing in the first-century, eastern Mediterranean world (Hanson and Oakman 1998; Malina 1993; Pilch 1991c).

What is the result? Medical anthropology, like all anthropological study, could help the exegete to adopt a transcultural stance, "a perceptual stance and research posture that is detached or 'alienated' but equidistant from two or more cultural units, however they may be defined" (Weidman 1988: 261–62). One of these cultural units is the investigator's own.

From this position, the exegete could choose to become a culture broker, that is, one who helps others understand cultures other than their own. The next step is to help people adopt a third culture rooted in expanded cross-cultural understanding. The process of developing a third culture entails first knowing one's own culture well, then recognizing the differences of the other culture. After learning to empathize with those differences, the exegete works at creating the common ground necessary for intercultural communication, that is, for answering the question: What does it mean for us? (Stewart and Bennett 1991: 16).

AFTERWORD

This chapter was originally prepared for presentation in the Historical Jesus Section at the annual meeting of the Society of Biblical Literature in Washington, D.C., in November, 1993. It was intended as a basic guide for non-specialists, specifically for biblical scholars, who were interested in investigating the healing activities of Jesus and other ancient figures. For further information and related links, the reader could consult the Web site of The Society for Medical Anthropology <www.people.memphis.edu/~sma>.

Jesus healing the leper
Egbert Codex, fol. 21 v, 10th century
Stadtbibliothek, Trier, Germany

3

SELECTING AN APPROPRIATE
MODEL: LEPROSY—A TEST CASE

MEDICALLY "ABSURD!" That's how Arthur Johnson, leprologist and director
of the Regional Hansen's Disease Center for Florida and Georgia, evaluated
the biblical reports of leprosy. From a medical point of view, of course,
Johnson is correct. The detailed description of leprosy in Leviticus 13–14
does not list any characteristic of true leprosy or Hansen's disease, as it is
known to modern medical science.

Many reports by modern patients to their physicians can also be described
as medically absurd. Indeed, some practitioners who realize how patients
tend to distort symptoms prefer to pay more attention to pathognomic tests
that can reveal the truth no matter what the patient may say (Feinstein
1973: 230).

But the Bible is not a medical textbook nor can the priests in Leviticus
be viewed like clinical practitioners. Van Hulse's suggestion (92) that Leviticus 13 can be considered a "more reasonable and understandable medical
document" if it is compared to that section of a chapter in modern medical
textbooks titled "Differential Diagnosis" is anachronistic and simply
wrong.

Medical anthropology urges modern scientific medical practitioners to
realize that there is more to reality than their "philosophy dreams of"
(Kleinman 1980; Good 1977; Good and Good 1981; Lewis 1981). The
reports of modern patients are not distortions that have to be decoded but
rather represent reality as the patient has constructed it. The biomedical
model of interpretation that dominates modern medical practice tends to
disregard such reports. In actuality this model needs to be supplemented
with a cultural model. The biomedical model, for example, is incapable of
appreciating ethnic or religious differences in interpreting human misfortune. For this task, a workable cultural model is proposed.

Many Bible interpreters who live in societies in which scientific Western medicine predominates accept the insights of biomedicine as the only valid interpretation of human sickness. When medical scientists like Johnson point out how medically absurd biblical descriptions of leprosy are, Bible interpreters unfortunately accept that statement and even accept the alternative diseases medical scientists propose (see, for example, Fitzmyer 1985: 573–74). In the end, of course, however the problem is correctly identified, the Bible insists that God or Jesus remedied it.

Because the cultural model of interpreting human sickness episodes has been developed particularly as an appropriate means of cross-cultural understanding, the cultural model of interpreting human sickness episodes can also serve as an appropriate model for interpreting biblical passages describing human sickness. Whether they recognize it or not, contemporary biblical scholars who attempt to interpret ancient texts from the Mediterranean world are engaged in a cross-cultural enterprise (Malina 1983). Any cross-cultural model for interpreting human sickness already validated in the medical domain can be an invaluable tool in the world of sacred texts as well.

To appreciate the contribution of a cultural or hermeneutic model for interpreting human sickness, it will be necessary first to reflect briefly upon the nature of models, and then to consider the biomedical or empiricist model. The cultural or hermeneutic model proposed by Byron and Mary Jo DelVecchio Good (1981) has been accepted and modified in this presentation for application to biblical texts.

MODELS: INTERPRETIVE TOOLS

A model is an abstract, simplified representation of more complex real-world objects and interactions (Malina 1993: 19). Physicians and laypersons use different models for interpreting human sickness conditions. The physician who uses the biomedical model believes that the symptoms the patient relates manifest some underlying biological reality, particularly some disordered somatic or psychophysiological process. The physician's challenge is to decode the patient's report and map it onto some disease. Adding this to independent observation, the physician seeks ultimately to convert observed evidence into names of diseases. The ultimate goal is to carry out rational treatment.

In this model, the flaky skin condition and underlying redness ("raw flesh" Lev. 13:9) reported in Leviticus needs to be decoded and mapped onto known diseases—for example, psoriasis, seborrhoeic dermatitis, patchy eczema, tinea, favus, etc. Only then could a modern physician begin to apply a rational treatment.

The layperson uses an implicit cultural model in integrating an illness into a meaningful human reality. The symptoms presented are not a code but rather condense in an appropriate idiom a series of personal tragedies. The flaky skin and underlying redness begin to make one stand out from the crowd. If declared unclean, such persons must remove themselves from the community and should be shunned (Lev 13:45-46). In collectivistic, that is, group-oriented societies, such excommunication is devastating. It is the equivalent of a death sentence. The words *leprosy* and *leper,* as used in the Bible, certainly carries these meanings above all.

Every model is selective; it concentrates on certain elements as important and ignores the others. The biomedical model focuses only on elements that can have biological significance. The cultural model looks for human meaning. The result is that each model perceives different symptoms, and each model constructs human sickness differently. Because each model has its own structure of relevance—that is, it makes relevant certain data or aspects of reality that are ignored or left unanalyzed by other models—it is beneficial to utilize a variety of models (Schutz 1970; Good and Good 1981: 177).

SEMANTIC NETWORKS

Human sickness as a personal and social reality and its therapy is inextricably bound to language and signification. The biomedical model depends upon an empiricist theory of language that believes that the order of words should reflect and reveal the order of things. If someone uses the word *leprosy,* that word should reveal "how the world as a matter of empirical fact functions and is constituted." The biblical use of 'leprosy' (whether in English, or the Hebrew or Greek counterparts) simply does not reflect the order of medical things. Therefore, it has to be decoded. Notice that the relationship of disease to culture is two-dimensional: words and things (see Foucault 1970; White 1986).

In contrast, experience with modern ethnic groups and individuals has demonstrated that groups vary in the specificity of sickness complaints, the style of complaining in various healing contexts (McGoldrick et al. 1982; Zborowski 1969, 1952), the nature of anxiety about the meaning of systems, the focus on particular organ systems, and the response to therapeutic strategies (Zola 1966). The same holds true for the ethnic Mediterranean groups who appear on the pages of the Bible. Thus, the cultural or hermeneutic model seeks the connection between the words ('white spot' and 'raw flesh') and the things (parts of the body displaying such anomalies) and the human experience (unclean). Here the relationship of disease and culture is three-dimensional: words, things, and human meaning.

Human sickness, or illness, can thus be conceived as a coherent syndrome of meaning and experience that is linked to society's deep semantic and value structures. It should be obvious why medical anthropologists insist that the semantic structures of various illnesses provide the framework from which the interpretation of symptoms must begin (Good and Good 1981: 175, 177).

THE BIOMEDICAL OR EMPIRICIST MODEL

According to empiricism, the theoretical foundation of modern science, symptoms (aberrations or deviations from what is considered normal) manifest disordered somatic or psychophysical processes. Something has gone noticeably wrong with the body. A client comes to the physician and complains of a rash that will not go away, a loss of appetite, a recurring fever at night. In the empirical perspective, these symptoms signal to both the client and the practitioner that something is awry with or in the body.

The main task of the modern Western practitioner is to decode these symptoms and translate them into the name of a disease. The symptoms just mentioned could indicate eczema, fungus, skin cancer, or syphilis, among other things. Laboratory tests would have to be ordered; bodily systems would have to be checked out.

The therapist's goal is quite clear. The disease must be identified (diagnosed) and explained, the symptoms must be correctly related to the bodily disorder or disease. Then, of course, the therapist must intervene in the disease process to eradicate it or halt its progress.

In this case, a therapist in the contemporary United States might conceivably never think of leprosy. Only as additional symptoms come into play—such as a gradual loss of sensation, numbness—might the therapist think of running the simple test for leprosy. But this second set of symptoms can take as many as twenty years to manifest itself.

The biomedical or empirical model can be presented in its six basic steps; a sketchy application to Leviticus 13 will illustrate how it works:

1. Observe Pathological Entity
A bodily abnormality or dysfunction manifests itself, for example, *ṣaraʿat:* "swelling, eruption, spot, leprous disease" on the "skin of the body" (Lev. 13:2).

The Biomedical or Empiricist Model	The Cultural or Hermeneutic Model
1. Observe pathological entity. A bodily dysfunction manifests itself.	1. Pathological entity emerges: sufferer constructs a meaningful illness reality.
2. Seek relevant symptoms. Only those symptoms that "reveal" something about a known bodily disorder are relevant data.	2. Seek relevant data.
3. Conduct elicitation procedures: lab tests; review of bodily systems. Patient's report helpful but not necessary; technology reveals all.	3. Elicitation procedure; evaluate the patient's explanatory models (EMs) and decode the semantic illness network. Highly idiosyncratic for each individual.
4. Interpretive goal: diagnose and explain the symptoms.	4. Interpretive goal: understand the meaning this illness episode has for the patient; for benefit of the client.
5. Interpretive strategy: explore the relationship between symptoms and the bodily disorder, find the bodily referent of the symptom. "Rule out . . ."	5. Interpretive strategy: explore the relationship between symptoms and semantic illness network. Text (symptoms) and context (semantic illness network).
6. Therapeutic goal: intervene (with surgery, chemotherapy, or another technique or strategy) in the bodily disease process to eradicate it or to halt its progress.	6. Therapeutic goal: a therapist must treat the client's experience. "Bring to understanding the hidden aspects of the illness reality and transform that reality. Reformulate the client's self-understanding by establishing a meaningful context.

TABLE 3.1: Comparison between the Biomedical/Empiricist Model and the Cultural/Hermeneutic Model.

2. Seek Relevant Symptoms

Only those symptoms that reveal something about a known bodily disorder are relevant data. The Hebrew *ṣaraʿat* translated as 'leprosy' appears to describe a patchy skin condition. If it spread over the entire body it was not *ṣaraʿat* (Lev. 13:12-13). The sections that report that "whitened hair" are a sign of *ṣaraʿat* cannot refer to real leprosy (Hansen's disease), or any known skin disease (Lev. 13:18-20, 23, 24-28), because that symptom does not accompany such diseases.

3. Conduct Elicitation Procedures

Order a series of laboratory tests, a review of bodily systems. What the patient says may be helpful but not very important since the labwork finds, and the test results tell, all there is to know from the biomedical perspective (Feinstein 1973: 230). While labwork as such is impossible relative to biblical texts, paleopathology can be of some related assistance. Paleopathology, or the scientific examination of bones exhumed from ancient graves, when done in Egypt and Palestine have yielded only one (post-Christian!) case of leprosy in Egypt and none in Palestine (van Hulse 1975: 89–90). This evidence, together with the symptoms listed, argue strongly against the proposition that "real" leprosy is the concern in Leviticus or in the biblical world in general.

4. Interpretive Goal

Diagnose and explain the symptoms. What sense can one make of the biblical reports in Leviticus? What were the people called "lepers" (Hebrew *ṣarûʿ;* Greek *lepros*) who encountered Jesus suffering from?

5. Interpretive Strategy

Dialectically explore the relationship between the symptoms and the bodily disorder; find the bodily referent of a symptom. Contemporary physicians will listen to a patient's report, make a personal observation of the symptoms, then order a specific test with the phrase "Rule out hypoglycemia," or "Rule out diabetes." The order effectively means: "Prove my judgment wrong!" Carefully reviewing the symptoms presented in Leviticus 13 permits them to be mapped onto diseases such as psoriasis, seborrhoeic dermatitis, fungus infections of the skin (for example, tinea) but particularly favus, patchy eczema, and pityriasis rosea (van Hulse 1975: 96–97). Hansen's disease, real leprosy, is definitely ruled out.

6. Therapeutic Goal

The therapist next seeks to intervene in the disease process by means of surgery, chemotherapy, or another technique or strategy in order to eradicate the disease or halt its progress. This is obviously impossible in the case of biblical reports, but interpreters who apply this biomedical model of interpretation to biblical texts feel satisfied in having arrived at the medical truth and disproving leprosy or validating an alternative disease (see Rosner 1977; Bleich 1981).

It would seem that the biomedical model is of little use prior to the discovery of the biomedical cause of leprosy. People totally unaware of germs, viruses, and other microscopic pathogens would never be able to hit upon that answer. A physician from Bergen, Norway, Gerhard Henrik Armauer Hansen, first discovered the *mycobacterium leprae* in 1868 and described it in 1873–74. It was one of the first pathological organisms to be recognized. The leprosy germ is a bacillus, which means it is rod-shaped, about one six-thousandth of an inch long.

Several misconceptions about leprosy (Hansen's disease) persist in modern perception, but the disease is only mildly contagious. Rarely do spouses or children contract it, and it is not transmitted sexually. No one has ever died from leprosy; those who contract it have the same life-expectancy as anyone else. Nor do the fingers and toes rot and drop off. Rather, the disease deadens nerve endings, and with a lack of feeling, cuts and other sources of infection often go undetected until the infection spreads to the bones which in turn are gradually destroyed. Physical deformations do not occur unless the disease is untreated for fifteen or twenty years. Only two forms of leprosy can disfigure the skin with lesions and scales: lepromatous and tuberculoid.

With the absence of these kinds of symptoms in biblical descriptions of leprosy, it is no wonder that scientists call the relevant chapters medically absurd. The surprise is that professional Bible interpreters who accept the judgment still wrestle with explaining how the cure of this new problem took place. The cultural or hermeneutic model can shed important light on what is transpiring in such an event.

THE CULTURAL OR HERMENEUTIC MODEL

Meaning-centered medical anthropology has devised a cultural or hermeneutic model to assist contemporary health professionals in making conscious translations of health problems across meaning systems in order to understand the realities perceived by others. Since this kind of enterprise is precisely what contemporary Bible interpreters and readers are constantly doing, such models would be of special value to biblical scholars and biblical readers (Pilch 1981a; see also chapter 2 of this book).

Such an approach rests on two basic assumptions. First, all illness realities are fundamentally semantic. Sickness becomes a human experience and an object of therapeutic attention when it becomes meaningful. Physicians make sickness meaningful by identifying the disease that fits the symptoms. Laypeople make sickness meaningful in a very subjective way, drawing upon a wide range of knowledge and ultimately constructing an illness. Thus illness realities will differ widely from individual to individual within a society, culture, or ethnic group. Second, all healing is a fundamentally hermeneutic

or interpretive activity. The patient's symptoms and identified illness represent personal and group values and conceptualizations and are not simply
biological reality. The illness reality is completely subjective, a "patch of personal biography" (Lewis 1981: 156).

Thus, the process of healing involves understanding the culturally specific illness reality created by the patient, and then directing therapeutic efforts to transform those realities (Good and Good 1981: 177; Kleinman
1980). Healing is essentially an interpretive activity carried out according to
the specific interpretive strategies adopted by the healer. A biomedical
model is constrained by the biomedical principles, but a cultural or
hermeneutic model should be able to discern the unique strategies of healers as well as the unique illness realities constructed by patients even if they
suffer from the same named malady.

The cultural or hermeneutic model contains the same six elements as the
biomedical model but in a different way. Because this model allows for
cross-cultural understanding, it can be applied to the interpretation of biblical leprosy as well as other biblical reports of illness with a greater degree of
cultural plausibility.

1. Pathological Entity Emerges

A person notices the appearance of a physical abnormality on the body,
mainly affecting the skin. The culture guides that person to construct a
meaningful illness out of that reality. In English translations of the Bible,
this reality is called leprosy (Hebrew, ṣara'at; Greek, lepra).

2. Seek Relevant Data

What kinds of data reveal or manifest the meaning of the illness? What are
the semantics of the illness? Biblical leprosy is always considered an unclean
condition. Leviticus 13–14 repeatedly note that the ultimate judgment to be
made by the priests after examining the person is: clean or unclean. In the
New Testament, lepers ask to be declared or made clean in all the texts except
Luke 17:12, which has 'healed'—though some manuscripts have 'cleansed.'
Leviticus 13:45-46 decrees that an unclean person had to live "outside the
camp." In the New Testament, lepers seem to have been in the village (Luke
17:12) and appear to have had easy access to non-afflicted persons, such as
Jesus. Part of the therapeutic process involves "showing one's self to the
priest" and/or "offering what Moses commanded" if declared clean.

The appeal to Jesus to "have mercy" (Luke 17:13) suggests the condition
elicited no compassion from others. No doubt it entailed aversion and perhaps even rejection. The words and phrases "clean/unclean," "showing one's

self to the priests," and "offering what Moses commanded," together with the fact that the leper-petitioners had easy access to Jesus, strongly suggest the issue is pollution rather than contagion. This is how that culture construed this illness in a humanly meaningful way. They had no way of knowing about diseases caused by unseen bacteria.

3. Elicitation Procedure

The next step is to evaluate the patient's explanatory models (EMs) and decode the semantic illness network. An EM, as noted earlier, is an array of notions about an illness episode and its treatment (see Kleinman 1980: 104–6). Everyone involved in the healing process uses an EM, but clearly not the exact same one. An EM is personal and highly idiosyncratic for each participant in the process. Essentially, EMs seek to answer five major questions for each illness episode: cause or origin; time and mode of onset of symptoms, pathophysiology, course of the sickness (degree of severity, type of sick role, etc.), and treatment.

This is clearly a professional statement of the model from a biomedical perspective. To determine a layperson's EM, one would ask questions like these: (1) What do you call your problem? What name does it have? (2) What or who do you think has caused your problem? (3) Why do you think it started when it did? (4) What does your sickness do to you? How does it work? (5) How severe is it? Will it last a long or a short time? (6) What do you fear most about your sickness? (7) What are the chief problems your sickness has caused for you? (8) What kind of treatment do you think you should receive? What are the most important results you hope to receive from the treatment? (9) How has your family and community reacted to you since the onset of your problem?

By using the following list to massage the biblical accounts of lepers seeking help, it is possible to put biblical leprosy in fresh perspective.

1. The afflicted person is invariably called a leper or described as being "covered with leprosy."

2. The cause of this problem (in the New Testament or in Leviticus) is not identified. It must be remembered, however, that peasants in the ancient Mediterranean world did not recognize secondary causality. Every event had to have a *personal* cause. If the problem was not caused by a human person, then one might suspect an other-than-human person. Thus, illness could be God's punishment for sin (Num. 12:6-9; John 5:14)—though not necessarily so (John 9:3)—or God's way of drawing people to true fear of the Lord (Job 33:19-33). Stories of demon possession are clearly caused by some malevolent spirit.

3. There is no way to tell why the problem occurred when it did.

4. Two effects of this skin problem that seem to loom large in both the Old and New Testaments is that it classified people as unclean and consequently deprived them of social interaction and participation. An afflicted person had to be separated from the community.

5. The severity of the problem in biblical accounts appears to be located in the stigma and consequences of being labeled unclean. This is highly significant because, from a biomedical perspective, true leprosy is neither dirty nor unclean nor does it necessarily require isolation or quarantine.

6. The biggest fear deriving from this kind of a situation is that the afflicted person may never be able to return to the community.

7. Exclusion from the community is the chief problem this malady causes. For socio-centric or collectivistic persons (who constitute 80 percent of the contemporary population of the planet and perhaps an even greater percentage in antiquity), this is a major problem.

8. Small wonder, then, that the request to Jesus in almost every instance is "make me clean" (in Luke 7:13 the request is for "mercy/compassion/ pity"). The expected result in either case is a return to full membership in the community.

Efforts to decode the semantic network appear to produce the same conclusion. Each illness reality is constituted as a unique semantic network. The report in Matt. 8:1-4//Mark 1:40-45 //Luke 5:12-15 concerns a leper, a man covered with leprosy. He requests to be made clean, if Jesus wills that. The result of Jesus' concurrence is that his leprosy is cleansed (Matt.), it leaves him (Mark, Luke), or he is "made clean" (Mark). Jesus declares him clean and sends him to the priest for verification and official pronouncement that he is clean. As a result, he should "offer the gift that Moses commanded," which can only take place within the community place of worship. That act of thanksgiving is confirmation of the reality of the new condition.

Luke 17:11-19 seems patterned after the cleansing of Naaman in 2 Kings 5:9-15 (Hobbs 1985: 55–69, 292). The afflicted lepers request mercy or pity from Jesus. This might *not* imply a request for a cleansing so much as a request for human compassion and momentary fellowship. The narrative, however, says they were cleansed (v. 13) and/or healed (v. 15, though some manuscripts read "cleansed" here, too). Jesus' final comment to the one who returned to thank and praise God is: "your faith [best understood in the Mediterranean world as loyalty] has saved you." Presumably the other nine were also delivered by loyalty and perhaps even praised God, but they did not return to Jesus. The semantic illness network in this story highlights compassion and deliverance (traditionally spoken of as "salvation") or rescue from an undesirable situation along with the cleansing as elements desired by the petitioners.

Decoding semantic illness networks demands that the analyst focus on group conceptualizations and values, and strive to discover the deep personal meanings associated with an illness or a symptom. The overarching concern to be clean or cleansed can be related to the command so often repeated in Leviticus 17–26 (the so-called Holiness Code): "You must be holy, for I, Yahweh your God, am holy" (19:2). This segment follows after a discussion of "clean and unclean" or "holy and not-holy" situations in Leviticus 11–15. Obviously anyone suffering a leprosy illness was not holy like the Lord. This is the key group conceptualization and value that underlie the individual, deep personal meanings associated with leprosy in biblical accounts.

In the New Testament, Jesus echoes the charge of Leviticus even as he modifies it: "You must be perfect [whole], as your heavenly Father is perfect [whole]" (Matt. 5:48); and "Be merciful [compassionate], even as your Father is merciful [compassionate]" (Luke 6:36). What a perfectly sensible implication Luke's Jesus makes here! To be perfect like God is to imitate God's compassion as well. Luke's lepers may have planned a deliberate strategy to see if Jesus would practice what he preached and show them the mercy or compassion withheld by others. Jesus did not fail to meet their expectations.

4. The Interpretive Goal: Understanding

Recall that the biomedical model seeks to make a diagnosis; it needs to know the symptoms quite precisely and specifically so that the malady can be mapped onto the physical body of the person and rational therapy can be initiated. To call the biblical narratives about leprosy medically absurd is a failure to understand the client's reality. The cultural or hermeneutic model is concerned rather with understanding the meaning this illness episode has for the patient, whence the name "hermeneutic."

5. The Interpretive Strategy

Here the purpose is to explore the relationship of symptoms and semantic illness network. These stand in relationship to one another as text (symptoms) and context (semantic illness network). With regard to a leper's illness episodes, how does the flaky and repulsive skin condition (leprosy) relate to the personal feeling of being unclean and the strong desire to be cleansed or pronounced clean?

The human body is a symbolic reality that bridges the personal world with the socio-cultural world. According to Mary Douglas (1966: 115):

The human body is a model which can stand for any bounded system. Its boundaries can represent any boundaries which are threatened or precarious. The body is a complex structure. The functions of its different parts and their relations afford a source of symbols for other complex structures. We cannot possibly interpret rituals concerning excreta, breast milk, saliva, and the rest unless we are prepared to see in the body a symbol of society, and to see the powers and dangers credited to social structures reproduced in small on the human body.

The rules in Leviticus 11–15 listing and explaining why certain things are clean and unclean touch four major categories: clean and unclean animals (11); childbirth or uncleanness similar to menstruation (12); unclean skin (a scaly or flaky condition), garments, and walls (13-14); and unclean bodily discharges, such as semen and blood (15). These specific chapters are considered to derive from the post-exilic era (after 537 B.C.E.) or approximately contemporaneous with Ezra's determination to restore holiness to the community by dissolving marriages with foreign women (Ezra 10:10-11). Society was deeply concerned about being holy like the Lord is holy and purifying marriages seemed one way to restore and maintain a holy community.

How does biblical leprosy fit into this context? Douglas (1966: 113) notes that all pollution, for example, biblical leprosy,

> is a type of danger which is not likely to occur except where the lines of structure, cosmic or social, are clearly defined. . . . When rituals express anxiety about the body's orifices, the sociological counterpart of this anxiety is a care to protect the political and cultural unity of a minority group. The Israelites were always in their history a hard pressed minority. In their belief all the bodily issues were polluting: blood, pus, excreta, semen, etc. The threatened boundaries of their body politic would be well mirrored in their care for the integrity, unity, and purity of the physical body.

In Leviticus, three topics relate to bodily openings or orifices: clean and unclean foods (mouth); childbirth/menstruation (female genitals); bodily discharges (male and female genitals). The repulsive flaky condition (leprosy) also affects boundaries: skin, garments (a secondary skin boundary), and walls. There is a concern, therefore, about unusual or abnormal openings on these boundaries. Note the repeated concern to determine whether a blemish is "deeper than the skin of the body." Such openings on the skin signal a weak body boundary and pose risks to the holiness of the body.

Again Douglas comments (1966: 4): "So also can the processes of ingestion portray political absorption. Sometimes bodily orifices seem to represent points of entry or exit to social units, or bodily perfection can symbolize an ideal theocracy."

The point is that the community and its members are expected to be holy because God is holy (Lev. 11:44-45). Ezra "cleansed" the community by dissolving marriages between Israelites and foreigners. To further strengthen the pure or clean community and replicate the law of society in individual life, the rules concerning foods, births, and flaky or weak body-boundary conditions were gathered in Leviticus 11–15, promulgated and enforced. The rules governing boundaries of the social body were replicated and reinforced on the physical body, and vice versa.

Accepting this understanding of biblical leprosy as the context, how does an interpreter approach the instances in healing leprosy in the New Testament?

Matthew 8:1-4//Mark 1:40-45//Luke 5:12-15. In each of these passages, which relate the same event, the afflicted one (leper) requests Jesus to "make him clean" and Jesus obliges. He says: "I will [it]; be [made] clean!" The theological passive voice indicates that God is the agent who cleansed the afflicted ones. Jesus declared the petitioner clean, that is, acceptable and welcome in the community. Jesus extended the boundaries of society and included in the holy community many who were otherwise excluded (lepers, tax collectors, prostitutes).

Each version is told in straightforward fashion and is interpreted more by position in the respective Gospel than by content. Mark uses the story to illustrate the power and authority with which Jesus taught. (Kazmierski's analysis of this version is complete and masterful.) Matthew's story is the first in a cluster of ten presented in the context of discipleship. This is similar to Luke, who tells the story to illustrate the source and non-exclusiveness of discipleship.

The social significance of the successful remedy is more important than the report itself or the fact. Kleinman (1980: 82) notes: " 'Cultural healing' may occur when healing rites reassert threatened values and arbitrate social tensions. Thus therapeutic procedures may heal social stress independent of the effect they have on the sick person who provides the occasion for their use." The interpretive strategy of placing this story of Jesus' healing the leper into the wider context of biblical leprosy certainly shows the concern is not contagion but pollution, an integral part of the Judean social system (Malina 1993; 149–83; Neyrey 1986b). In none of the synoptic contexts is there a hint that the leper is quarantined. He seems to be in a public place, mingling with others, and has rather easy access to Jesus.

In each report Jesus is said to *touch* the leper. Aside from the facts that real leprosy is only mildly contagious (and the biblical reports are not talking about real leprosy anyway), touching is capable of multiple interpretations. Touching is the way power is transmitted, so that Jesus' touch is an effective conduit for healing power. But perhaps in these instances the touching draws significance not so much from showing no fear of pollution but from physically symbolizing an acceptance back into the community. After all, the expulsion was for reasons of pollution not contagion. The presence of a leprous person in the camp polluted the camp. Jesus' touching is a concrete way of demonstrating that the individual is a full member of the community as Jesus understands it.

In Mark 7:1-13 (//Matt. 15:1-20) Jesus challenges the notion that pollution and danger exists beyond the boundaries, somewhere out there, whence derives the demand for ritual washing of hands and utensils. Rather, Jesus says, the threat to holiness, the danger of pollution, is located within the community itself. Thus does Jesus reassert threatened values (the continued existence of a holy community) and arbitrate social tensions (who is in and who is out of the community).

Luke 17:11-19. Read this passage along with 2 Kings 5:9-15. In this story, ten lepers approach and beg: "Jesus, Master, have mercy on us." Note that they do not request cleansing or healing, though it is plausibly implied. In Mediterranean culture, to request mercy is to say to that person: "Do what you owe me!" "Behave according to your status and abilities." Jesus' reply is that they go and show themselves to the priests who, according to the Law, would examine them to determine whether their condition was clean or unclean. It is on the journey that they were cleansed. The passive voice is a "theological" passive: God is responsible for the cleansing. Jesus effectively intervened as a broker with God the Patron on behalf of these clients (Malina 1988).

One of the ten came back to give praise to God and thank Jesus. The text says he was healed (Greek *iathē*), though some manuscripts report cleansed *(ekatharisthē);* Fitzmyer (1985: 1155) correctly notes that the sense is not affected. The petitioner realized that his condition was now clean and no longer unclean. In the cultural context it was improper to say "Thank you." This phrase willingly signals the end of the relationship. A Middle Eastern proverb states: "Don't thank me; you will repay me." The person who thanked Jesus was a foreigner, one who was not of Jesus' group. He knew his chance of ever encountering this non-Samaritan again was slight—hence his willingness to terminate the relationship. Jesus' fellow Judeans might need Jesus' help again, since no healings were forever.

Jesus' final comments about giving praise to God and about the saving nature of faith/loyalty is very likely Luke's creation, since 17:1-19 is organized around the question: What is faith? It forgives (vv. 1-4); it can do all things (vv. 5-6); it is humble (vv. 7-10); and it is grateful to the proper person (vv. 11-19). The story of the ten lepers who received compassion and cleansing is reshaped to highlight the point of gratitude.

Placing this story into the wider context of biblical leprosy makes the lepers' request for mercy stand out as significant. They came to Jesus believing he could help in some way—even if only to show compassion—and that faith proved effective for all of them.

6. The Therapeutic Goal

Whereas in the biomedical model a therapist intervenes in the somatic process, in the cultural model a therapist must treat the client's experience. The healer strives to "bring to understanding hidden aspects of the illness reality and to transform that reality" (Good and Good 1981: 179). In other words, the therapist strives to reformulate the patient's self-understanding by establishing a meaningful context.

In the New Testament leper stories, the clients' experiences of being unclean or being deprived of mercy/compassion/pity were presented to Jesus. The illness-reality that Jesus transforms is the notion of impurity/uncleanness or a sense of not finding mercy/compassion/pity and its effect on membership in the holy community. His actions result in establishing a new meaningful context that does indeed reformulate the petitioner's self-understanding—from unclean to clean, from undeserving of compassion to finding mercy, pity, and compassion (Lipowski 1969).

Contemporary medical anthropologists note that a therapist's ability to influence a patient's reality and to help construct new realities not only combats demoralization but is in itself a powerful healing force (Frank 1974; Kleinman and Sung 1979). This seems certainly to be true of Jesus' healing activity in the Gospels.

CONCLUSION

The utilization of interpretive models for the treatment of individuals is basic to all healing activity. Two interpretive models were considered here: the biomedical or empiricist, and the hermeneutic or cultural. Because the biomedical model depends too heavily on modern, scientific understandings of human sickness as disease, it is less helpful in interpreting healing accounts from antiquity. The hermeneutic model is much better suited to analyzing human illness experiences across cultures. This makes it a helpful and indispensable tool for anyone interested in interpreting the various healing stories in the Bible. Indeed the hermeneutic model urges that any analysis of healing should begin with the interpretive strategy of the healer.

AFTERWORD

An additional perspective might be added to this discussion of leprosy or other illnesses mentioned in the New Testament. Leprosy in the New Testament period might have become a culture-bound syndrome (see chapter 2 above, and Simons and Hughes 1985). The emphasis on clean and unclean dimensions of life, membership in or exclusion from community, and the requirement of avoiding liaisons with foreigners, all these emerged in the post-exilic period and grew stronger with each successive conquest and domination by another world power: Persia, Greece, Rome. It would be interesting to investigate whether Hansen's disease ever attracted such meanings in other instances, or whether other cultures created or reinterpreted a given physical condition to reflect concern about avoiding contact or intermingling with foreigners.

Jesus healing the possessed man
Egbert Codex, fol. 26 v., 10th century
Staadtbibliothek, Trier, Germany

4

HEALING IN MARK

IN THE FIRST VOLUME of *A Marginal Jew,* John P. Meier explains that he
does not intend to use "formal sociological analysis (or the cross-cultural
analysis of anthropology)" in his study (1991: 10). When discussing Jesus'
healings in the second volume, Meier correctly notes that "since the
Gospel healing stories do not make neat distinctions in their vocabulary
for healing," neither will he (1994: 728). Given the challenge every "outsider"—especially an anthropologist—faces when visiting an alien culture,
one wonders how Meier can be certain he has truly grasped the native
perspective in the documents he examines. Undeterred and seemingly
unaware of this challenge, he then proceeds to categorize and analyze
Jesus' healings without defining what healing might mean. In a footnote,
he recommends the social-scientific study of Mark, which follows in this
chapter, to readers interested in this approach.

Biblical scholars who utilize social-scientific methods and models to
interpret ancient documents from cultures other than their own consider
these documents as a kind of field report (Malina 1983). Even though the
documents may be modified or skewed by each respective tradition, author,
or redactor, it would be most helpful if a researcher knew the fundamental
values of Mediterranean culture so as to better appreciate how the author or
redactor is manipulating that information to some given purpose. One representative medical anthropologist offers a helpful insight when she points
out that the social sciences can serve as "tools of data retrieval" (Ohnuki-
Tierney 1981: 9). She admits to a passion for regularities and seeks "patterns and structures." All social scientists seek these very same things,
though they follow different paths.

The patterns and structures the investigator seeks are often not purely
hypothetical but rather based on the results of many earlier investigations

that have contributed to the identification of regularities that seem to be present in many cultures. Though details differ and the pattern may be nuanced, the rough outline remains recognizably the same across many cultures.

Until recently, biblical exegetes have relied on linguistic and literary tools for combing New Testament data in search of patterns and structures that might confirm or enrich their understanding of various passages. Now increasing numbers of scholars draw upon a variety of social science methods to supplement and enhance the other exegetical tools. Though still debated by some, the legitimacy of social-scientific approaches has been sufficiently argued elsewhere to be adopted in this study without further justification (Malina, 1983). In a survey of contemporary methods and approaches toward interpreting the Bible, the Pontifical Biblical Commission included a section on the use of the human sciences (sociology, cultural anthropology, psychological and psychoanalytical approaches) and gave qualified but favorable approval (1993).

The specific sub-branch of medical anthropology that is especially relevant to biblical research is ethnomedicine or comparative ethnomedicine. The *International Encyclopedia of the Social Sciences* defines comparative ethnomedicine as: "those beliefs and practices relating to disease which are the products of indigenous cultural development and are not explicitly derived from the conceptual framework of modern medicine" (Hughes 1968: 99).

Ethnomedicine places primacy on the culturally construed causes of illness. It views medical problems as sociocultural phenomena and therefore as culturally definable. In contrast, biomedicine places primary emphasis on biological symptoms and pathogens, whether or not the person is even aware of them. Biomedicine views health problems as universal and objective phenomena capable of being defined in the abstract. Thus, "a category of cancer, defined in terms of etiology in biomedicine, simply does not exist in non-biomedical traditions. A tuberculosis in biomedicine may be equivalent to several illnesses in another medical system" (Ohnuki-Tierney 1981: 11).

Moreover, the form of biomedicine that has developed in Western societies contains so much of the Western cultural tradition that it must be thoroughly reviewed and these Western elements sifted out before it can serve as an "outsider" framework of analysis. The challenge to Western exegetes is to realize that the specific Western understanding of human health problems in which they have been socialized in their given cultural setting often accounts for posing biomedical questions to the pre-scientific, ancient, Mediterranean New Testament documents. Such questions are not only irrelevant, but also erroneous.

Anthropologists use two terms that are peculiar to their field and require some effort to learn since they have no etymology, but were borrowed from the words *phonetic* and *phonemic* (Pike 1969). The terms are: etic and emic. *Etic* describes an outsider perspective on reality, while *emic* describes an insider perspective, the "native viewpoint" (see Pilch 1997 for the way these two viewpoints work in tandem). In biblical texts, there is a reality that the Judeans describe as demon-possession (an emic viewpoint) and that some modern interpreters identify as epilepsy or mental illness (an etic viewpoint) (Hollenbach 1982).

In other words, the New Testament documents are emic, and interpreters create etic models to understand that reality. The contemporary believer's penchant for relevance—an outsider's search for meaning in these insiders' texts—requires that the investigation move "from etic to emic and back to etic again." Only in this way can these documents be relevant to us, to our culture and experience (Malina 1981: 1307).

Analysis of the emic data (the New Testament documents) can proceed along two lines: rational and empiricist. A rational analysis focuses on language and seeks the structure of ideas in the unconscious. It looks at the individual as the actor and the focal point. An empiricist analysis, on the other hand, focuses on behavior. It observes the transaction and strives to relate it to the sociocultural structure. As is often the case in anthropological research, the best procedure is to combine both analytical methods.

Finally, the specific aspect of interest in this investigation is the etic concepts of sickness, disease, and illness. From the medical anthropological perspective, sickness is viewed as a blanket term for the reality, while disease and illness are two explanatory concepts for understanding that single reality (Kleinman 1980: 72). Disease derives from a biomedical perspective that sees abnormalities in the structure and/or function of organ systems. These are pathological states independent of whether or not they are culturally recognized. Disease affects individuals, and only individuals are treated. Illness, on the other hand, derives from a sociocultural perspective that is concerned with personal perception and experience of certain socially disvalued states that include, but are not limited to, disease. Illness inevitably affects others: the significant other, the family, the neighborhood, the village.

The sickness described in the Old Testament as leprosy is not leprosy at all from a biomedical perspective. But from a sociocultural perspective—which is what the Bible always reports—this condition called leprosy threatens communal integrity and holiness and must be removed from the community (see chapter 3 above; also Pilch 1981a).

Allan Young proposes a more refined understanding of sickness. It is not really a blanket term for disease/illness but "a *process* for socializing disease and illness," a process through which worrisome behavioral and biological signs, particularly ones originating in disease, are given socially recognizable meanings; that is, they are made into symptoms and socially significant outcomes (Young 1982: 270).

Finally, the etic understanding of the management of sickness takes two forms: curing and healing. A therapist who takes effective control of disordered biological and psychological processes is said to cure disease. In contrast, a therapist who provides personal and social meaning for the life problems created by sickness is said to heal illness. Thus, in modern medicine where both possibilities exist, the cure of disease is rare, but the healing of illness takes place always, infallibly, since everyone ultimately finds some meaning to given life situations: accidents, fate, will of God, providence, etc. (Kleinman 1980: 82). In our ancient, biblical documents, there is no interest in disease but only in illness.

The interrelationship between these various notions can be charted thus:

Etic   Disease   Biomedicine (distinctive Western medicine) with an interest in causes.

Emic   Illness   Sociocultural perspective with an interest in symptoms, classification, and social interpretation.

It is important to remember that these etic terms (sickness, disease, illness, cure, heal) should correctly and appropriately describe the emic reality reported by the people who populate the pages of the Bible. As defined here, these words do not appear in the translations. Where they do appear, they are drawn from dictionary definitions of Hebrew or Greek terms. A dictionary of Hebrew and Greek (emic) terms that would make an attempt to mesh with medical anthropological understanding (etic terms) would likely look like Louw and Nida's dictionary based on semantic domains. If future revisions of Louw and Nida would pay closer attention to the Mediterranean culture from which the Greek terms they discuss derive their meanings, modern scholars would be a step closer to attaining correct and plausible etic/emic relationships.

The Judeans, of course, would neither recognize the words we are using nor use them in the same way. Indeed, they apparently use the words *heal* and *cure* interchangeably, and not at all the way medical anthropologists use them. But if we were to discuss with them our understanding of reality behind the terms, and if our assessment is correct, they would agree with our conclusion.

THE HEALTHCARE SYSTEM

"The overwhelming distortion in medical anthropology . . . has been one in which healers were studied in isolation as the central component of medicine in society" (Kleinman 1980: 205). It would seem that the same could be said of biblical studies. In New Testament investigations, Jesus is obviously the focus but nearly always in isolation. Comparisons with other healers or healing traditions is often only for the purpose of highlighting the uniqueness of the person and activity of Jesus. To my knowledge, only one scholar (Avalos 1999) has attempted to delineate and explore the healthcare system of the New Testament world as I have done (Pilch 1985a).

Patients and healers exist within a cultural construct known as a *healthcare system*. This is where the analysis of healers must begin, for it is the whole system that heals, not just the healer (Kleinman 1980: 72). It is also important to note that a healthcare system is a concept, not an entity. It is a conceptual model held by the researcher (Kleinman 1980: 25). A model, following Geertz, is like a map of a special area of human behavior. The model is derived from observing particular societies and gradually coming to understand how people in a particular social setting think about, act in, and use the healthcare system. Obviously people's behavior is based on beliefs which are conditioned by cultural rules. Hence, a healthcare system is a cultural system and should be analyzed as such (Mackintosh 1978).

The healthcare system is not only cultural but also societal in origin, structure, function, and significance (Kleinman 1980: 27). In other words, it is created by a collective view and shared pattern of usage operating on a local level, but seen and used somewhat differently by different social groups, families, and individuals (Kleinman 1980: 39).

This suggests that each evangelist very likely has in mind a healthcare system with which he interprets the traditions he uses. This system is the one generally recognizable and acceptable to his audience even if his account nuances the features of the original report. In other words, the event as it happened at Level 1 (the lifetime of Jesus) is still available in the event as nuanced in the evangelist's report at Level 3 (Level 2 refers to the oral tradition).

The system can be viewed at a macro-level (whole societies or regions) or at a micro-level (localities: communities, neighborhoods, groups of families). This study will attempt the micro-level perspective, assuming that is what the evangelist is reporting.

The model proposed by Kleinman (see the accompanying diagram, p. 26) has three overlapping sectors: professional, popular, and folk. This is the inner structure of healthcare systems, which are roughly the same across cultural boundaries. The content, of course, varies with the social, cultural, and environmental circumstances of each system (Kleinman 1980: 48–49).

A final word of caution about the healthcare system: the very idea of such a system may well be an etic imputation by the investigator. Thus, the best approach is to see if empirical analysis does in fact turn up a system. There will often be overlap in the divisions of a system, and a society or culture can have more than one healthcare system (Worsley 1982: 320). Perhaps it is best to speak of a plurality of healthcare systems while focusing on local social systems as they relate to a wide variety of variables (Kleinman 1980: 35) (see Figure 2.1).

THE PROFESSIONAL SECTOR

This is the sector encompassing the organized healing professions, or the indigenous professionalized healers. Modern readers must use this word with care. Of course, professional healers in the modern sense did not exist in antiquity. Yet it is probably appropriate to identify as professional healers that category of persons who used methods and materials in healing that were not available in the popular or folk section. Casting this net over the biblical data does not turn up much information, but some definite notions are generally known and acknowledged.

OLD TESTAMENT

In the biblical world, the sentiment of Exodus 15:26 dominates: "I am the Lord, your healer." God is responsible for making people sick as well as for healing them. Prophets like Elijah (1 Kings 17) and Elishah (2 Kings 5) are credited with healing, but they did not belong to a professional healing class.

A passage dealing explicitly with what might be identified as a professional sector of healers is Sirach 38. On its face, the passage seems ambivalent toward professional physicians. It advises consulting this healer but reminds the client that the power to heal comes from God, who is still responsible for success or failure of the venture. Thus, Sirach advises:
   1. honoring the physician: vv. 1-8
      ♦ 38:1 "honor him before he is needed, for Lord created him."
   2. noting that both patient and physician rely on God:
      ♦ 38:12 "give the physician his place, for Lord created him . . . there is also need of him" (in addition to prayer, repentance, purification, and offerings).
      ♦ 38:13 "there is time when success lies in the physician's hands."

+ 38:14 "for he too will pray to the Lord to make his diagnosis successful, and cause his treatment to save life."
3. Criticism? not really:
   + 38:15 "he who sins before his maker may he fall into the
     care/hands of a physician!" or more likely (Hebrew text): "a sinner
     will resist his maker."
4. Above all remember: The Lord is healer!
   + 38:2 "healing comes from the Most High."
   + 38:9 "pray to the Lord and he will heal you."

In the second and first centuries before the common era when Sirach was
written, the Judean tradition was learning about the professional healing
groups in Hellenistic culture with curiosity and admiration. Sirach attempted to promote respect for tradition while not entirely squelching the
opportunities for learning from Hellenism (Noorda 1979: 215–24).

NEW TESTAMENT

The Greek word for 'physician' *(iatros)* appears only seven times in the New
Testament. A "Luke, beloved physician" is mentioned in Col. 4:14. Though
it is doubtful that this passage refers to Luke the evangelist, the individual
would appear to belong to the professional sector of the healthcare system.

The word also appears in the popular proverb quoted by Jesus (Mark
2:17//Matt. 9:12//Luke 5:31): "Those who are well have no need of a
physician, but those who are sick." Jesus speaks the proverb in reference to
himself, but it is not likely that he is identifying himself as a professional
physician. This kind of proverb referring to professional physicians is
found in many cultures (Carlston 1980: 99) and used rather broadly. In the
context, Jesus is defending his table fellowship with sinners and tax collectors. The proverb might draw more than is ordinarily recognized from a literal interpretation. If diseases are not the primary focus of healers in this
system, then illness—that is, life problems that relate to physical disorders
(disease) and more than that alone—could conceivably include one's
proper relationship with God (sinner) as well as proper relationships with
other citizens (tax collector). In other words, Jesus' friends are indeed
proper candidates for professional healers concerned with meaning in life.
Though not a professional healer himself, Jesus too has something to offer
regarding life's true purpose and meaning.

Yet another proverb is adduced by Jesus as a possible challenge to his
activity: "Doubtless you will quote to me this proverb: 'Physician, heal
yourself,' What we have heard you did at Capernaum do here also in your
own country" (Luke 4:23). The theme of the sick physician is common in

classical texts, and context always determines the meaning (Noland 1979: 193–209). The context in this case (even if it is not from Level 1) is cynicism, a "sign-seeking" that is not clear among the original audience but may have characterized the audience at another level (Fitzmyer 1981: 535).

Once again, the term *physician* is applied to Jesus in an analogous sense, much as it was applied to many individuals of that time. But the Lukan context also reports nothing about the healing activity of Jesus thus far, only his teaching. This association recurs in other passages (see folk sector below).

Finally, Mark 5:26//Luke 8:43 report the story of Jesus' healing of the woman with the menstrual irregularity. A common interpretation credits Mark with lambasting the professional medical sector, while Luke—presumed to be a professional physician—manifests the old-boy-network syndrome. The evangelist's identity as a physician is very dubious among modern biblical scholars. But beyond that, a consideration of these passages from the perspective of the healthcare system model suggests a plausible, alternative understanding. Mark indeed emphasizes the failure of the professional sector, but Luke does not so much defend physicians as he underscores the failure of all three sectors on behalf of this woman, who "could not be healed by anyone."

THE POPULAR SECTOR

This sector embraces the lay, non-professional, non-specialist popular culture. It is the largest part of any system, and its major interest is health and health maintenance, not sickness and cure. Ordinary people are concerned with leading a good life and doing whatever is necessary to avoid misfortune. In modern western parlance they lead a preventive lifestyle.

At the same time, this is the arena in which the misfortune is first labeled and defined, for only then can appropriate healing activities be initiated (Kleinman 1980: 50–53). The identification and labeling of the irregularity takes place within the several levels of this sector: individual, family, social network, and community beliefs. Let Mark's gospel serve as a focus for exploring the popular sector of the healthcare system in the biblical world.

THE INDIVIDUAL

It is important for the American exegete to realize that the American idea of the individual is quite different from that found in the biblical world.

Furthermore, the individual in American society is, from a global point of view, unique, and American society differs basically from many other societies. Here "the economic symbolism is structurally determining," whereas in most other societies "the locus of symbolic differentiation remains social relations," principally kinship relations, and other spheres of activity are ordered by the operative distinctions of kinship. Interpreting the individual in other societies, we cannot reproduce the individual in American society, for whom relationships with other humans are usually temporary and not ascribed—to be terminated at will. In American society, it is much easier for individuals to maximize their goal, because they are much freer from involvement with other human beings (Ohnuki-Tierney 1981: 16; see also Malina 1993: 63–89).

The people who appear in Mark's gospel are collectivistic or dyadic personalities, that is, individuals who depend heavily on the opinions and evaluations of others; they are socialized to intense group orientation rather than individualism. Such daily "checking out" by others heightens awareness of irregularities whenever they occur. Furthermore, the person's focus is on social relations or kinship (one of two formal social institutions among Mediterranean cultures of the first century C.E., the other being politics) (Hanson and Oakman 1998) rather than economics (a substantive social institution embedded in kinship and politics). This, too, affects the mode in which the popular sector of the healthcare system works. Recall that leprosy in the Bible was not Hansen's disease but rather conditions more like psoriasis and eczema. The concern of the community was not "public health" but social integrity, community holiness—an obvious and major concern in a society where kinship is a formal institution (see chapter 2).

The first therapeutic intervention resorted to by most people across a wide range of cultures is self-treatment (Kleinman 1980: 51). This ordinarily entails the following steps:

1. perceiving and experiencing symptoms
2. labeling and valuating the experience
3. sanctioning a particular kind of sick role: acute, chronic, impaired, medical, etc.
4. deciding what to do and engaging in specific healthcare-seeking behavior
5. applying treatment
6. evaluating the effect of self-treatment and therapy obtained from other sectors of the healthcare system (Kleinman 1980: 50–51).

What can this outline draw from biblical texts? Sirach 38 sums up the traditional as well as the new advice. Tradition urges praying to the Lord (v. 9), putting one's life in order (give up faults and sin, v. 10), and offering sacrifice (v. 11). These are the first steps in self-treatment. The new advice allows consulting a physician (professional sector, perhaps of Hellenistic orientation, v. 12) and using the medication proposed by the pharmacist (v. 4). Exploring the popular sector of the healthcare system at the level of the dyadic personality still further, it is interesting to note what irregularities affect the genders. Men in Mark's gospel are afflicted by unclean spirits, paralysis, a withered hand, deafness, a speech impediment, and blindness. All three symbolic zones of the Mediterranean human person are affected: hands-feet, heart-eyes, and mouth-ears (Malina 1993: 73–82). These misfortunes totally incapacitate a man—no zone is spared. The therapy will have to seek to restore wholeness.

Women in Mark are afflicted with unclean spirits, fever, death, and menstrual irregularity (hemorrhage). It is also interesting to note that most of the women are identified by their gender-determined status, role, or relationship: for example, mother-in-law, daughter. This is a normal mode of identifying people in Middle Eastern society (Abu-Lughod 1986). Moreover, this identification suggests that the misfortune has somehow deprived the household of a key person. The therapy restores the woman to a role that derives from the status. Peter's healed mother-in-law immediately begins to serve the houseguests, the role that usually belongs to the female status in the household.

The hemorrhaging woman is especially noteworthy since she symbolizes the power of womankind in the universal pattern in human society: public is to domestic as man is to woman. Menstrual blood is a positive symbol of women in the domestic domain, but taboo in the public domain. Jesus reins in her power-run-wild so she can once again assume a positive position in society (Ohnuki-Tierney 1981: 129–31).

FAMILY

We have little evidence about the kind of health maintenance or sickness care that was given at the family level. It is safe to guess that a sick dyadic individual would need "permission" from the family to assume the sick role, and would rely on family advice and help in the assessment of the sickness. Care at this level would of course include exhortation to pray and to admit one's sin (recall Job's friends). When these resources were exhausted, the family seems to have played some role in seeking care beyond the popular sector, from either the professional or the folk sector. They helped the sick person to seek out Jesus or some other healer.

Still, it is interesting to note that sick men do not seem to appear within an explicit family context, whereas women do. Sick men are in the synagogue (unclean spirit or withered hand) or in the company of others impersonally identified ("they" brought the paralytic [2:1-10] or deaf man [7:32] to Jesus). In actuality, these are a family context, more specifically, a fictive family context. The synagogue is a community center, and those who bring someone to Jesus are very likely fellow villagers and quite possibly family members. Thus, the characters in these contexts are very likely fictive kin if not actual kin from the extended family.

Women in this society are presumed to be part of some man (Malina 1993: 124) so it is normal and expected, for instance, that Jairus would plead for his daughter. It is also culturally expected that mothers might plead for their children (daughter with unclean spirit, 7:24-30). But it is out of the ordinary for a women to plead her own case. Notice that the hemorrhaging woman (5:25-34) only intends to touch Jesus' garment, but is then forced by circumstances to face him directly.

SOCIAL NETWORK

As kinship is one of the two formal social institutions in the New Testament world, it is expected that the social network might figure prominently in the popular sphere of the healthcare system. And indeed, it does. The "whole city" gathered at the door (1:33) when sick were brought to Jesus, and very likely the city was related through real or fictive kinship. The same may well be true of the deaf man with a speech impediment (7:32) and the blind man (8:22), who were both brought to Jesus by the impersonal "they."

Granted that some of these people were so incapacitated they needed the help of another, still the Good Samaritan (Luke 10:30-37) story reminds us that one had no reason to expect anything from anyone other than kin, real or fictive.

COMMUNITY BELIEFS AND PRACTICES

Medical anthropologists note that elements like sorcery, the evil-eye, and a powerful spirit world dominate Mediterranean belief systems (Murdoch 1980; Elliott 1988). The Gospel accounts of possession by demons or unclean spirits accurately reflect the social beliefs of the biblical world. Indeed, the description and classification as well as the naming of these spirits is available to us in many extra-biblical documents from the period of interest to exegetes (see for instance, *The Testament of Solomon;* Wink 1984). The modern interpreter shirks responsibility by failing to take this emic information seriously or worse yet dismissing it as unenlightened or primitive. Such basic community beliefs play a key role in identifying and classifying various sicknesses.

Furthermore, very practical consequences derive from these beliefs. The sick affected the entire village, hence they were of concern to the entire village. Not only did the populace gather at the door (1:33) where Jesus was healing, but it also determined that those, for instance, who suffered from the skin condition that they called leprosy should be quarantined away from the community. They surely knew that the condition they feared was not at all or very minimally contagious (even real leprosy is minimally contagious). It was their broader concern for community integrity that dictated the quarantine. Moreover, Jesus himself (or the healed person?) was asked to leave a neighborhood after a healing took place (5:17). One or the other for whatever reason was considered undesirable to the community.

TAXONOMY OF SICKNESS

Each sector of the healthcare system creates its own clinical reality (=the beliefs, expectations, norms, behaviors, and communicative translations) associated with sickness, healthcare seeking, practitioner-patient relationships, therapeutic activities, and evaluation of outcomes (Kleinman 1980: 42).

What kind of taxonomy (division) of sicknesses are evident in Mark's Gospel? Keep in mind we are discussing illness, that is, socioculturally constructed experiences. Thus, what exegetes have called interpretative contexts may well be a normal part of the total illness experience. Reading the Gospel of Mark with an eye to taxonomy uncovers a suggestive pattern in 1:29-34:

Mark 1:21	Jesus in synagogue	heals man with unclean spirit
Mark 1:29	Jesus in Peter's house	heals mother-in-law of fever
Mark 1:32-34	(summary)	they brought him all sick or possessed by demons; he healed many who were sick with various diseases and cast out many demons
Mark 1:39	(summary)	he went throughout Galilee preaching in their synagogues and casting out demons

TABLE 4.1: Pattern for Mark's illness taxonomy

A two-fold division seems to emerge in these passages: sickness, and affliction by unclean spirits or demons. In fact, it is possible to categorize the healing events in the remainder of Mark into one of the three divisions illustrated in Table 4.2.

Sickness	1:29-31 (mother-in-law's fever); 1:40-45 (leper); 2:1-12 (paralytic); 3:1-6 (withered hand); 5:21-24, 35-43 (dying daughter); 5:25-34 (hemorrhaging woman); 7:31-37 (deaf man/speech impediment); 8:22-26 (blind man); 10:46-52 (blind man).
Unclean Spirits or Demons	1:21-28 (man in synagogue); 3:20-30 (debate, Jesus accused "unclean spirit"); 5:1-20 (Gerasene); 7:24-30 (Syrophoenician daughter, unclean spirit/demon); 9:14-29 (14, 17, dumb; 15, deaf and dumb spirit); 9:38-40 (another casts out demons); 16:9-20 (Mary Magdalene; seven demons cast out; believers cast out demons).
Summary-Type Statements	1:32-34 (sick; demons); 1:39 (demons); 3:10-11 (diseases/unclean spirits); 6:5 (few sick people); 6:7-13 (disciples preach/authority over unclean spirits; cast out demons/anoint and heal); 6:53 (sick made well).

TABLE 4.2: Illness taxonomy in Mark

The illness episodes and their healing reported by Mark seem to fall into one of the two categories suggested by the various summary-type statements, especially those near the beginning of the Gospel. Jesus (and others) heal a wide variety of illnesses not involving demons or spirits, and they successfully cast out unclean spirits and demons where these beings are present.

George Foster proposed a division of medical systems into personalistic (human or divine agents involved) and naturalistic, based on etiology (in medicine: the causes or origins of a disease). Etiologies, however, are rarely mutually exclusive, though people tend to favor one or the other. The perspective of Sirach and that of the entire Bible suggests that the healthcare system reflected in them is personalistic. Such a system is never interested in, How did it happen? but rather, Who is responsible and why did it affect me? In the personalistic system of the Sakhalin Ainu where God permeates everything, Ohnuki-Tierney (1981: 37) uses the word *metaphysical* to describe illness in which the deity is considered to be involved, and *habitual* to describe illnesses in which no supernatural entity is involved.

Using the terms proposed by Foster (1976) and Ohnuki-Tierney, the taxonomy identified in Mark is thus mainly personalistic and reflects both habitual and metaphysical episodes. For Mark, though, I prefer to adhere more closely to the evidence and refer to illnesses not involving demons or spirits and illnesses that do involve demons or spirits.

Foster observes further: "In personalistic systems, illness is but a special case in the explanation of all misfortune" (1976: 776). Worsley similarly notes: "We are not dealing with illness but with misfortune and the prevention of misfortune" (1982: 327). From this perspective, one could broaden the taxonomy to include other misfortunes that may well belong very appropriately to the healthcare system. Thus, texts about misfortunes in which no demon or spirit is involved should include: hungry crowds (6:30-44; 8:1-9); clean/unclean perspective on well-being (7:1-23); fig tree (11:12-14, 20-21). Other narratives about misfortunes in which some kind of spirit or demon might be involved could be: storm of great wind (4:31-35); Peter/Satan (8:31-33).

What hitherto had been considered an interpretation of an illness episode by the evangelist may in fact be the normal and expected report of the Mediterranean sociocultural construction of the entire episode. Here bodily ills are taken to be mere epiphenomena, themselves material outcomes of immaterial forces and agencies that either inflict punishment for social misdeeds or act for no humanly intelligible reason at all.

Finally, the therapy in these accounts reflecting the popular sector of the healthcare system is beyond self-care, that is, beyond the ability of the afflicted one to cope with the affliction. To use the gospel language, the therapist cures/heals and/or casts out spirits. But in this connection it is interesting to note how often the healing/exorcising activity is associated with preaching/teaching (see 1:39; 6:5; 6:7, 13; 9:38). This association of teaching with healing in the activity of Jesus might be the best place to begin in exploring the folk sector of Mark's healing system.

FOLK SECTOR

The folk sector is the non-professional, non-bureaucratic, specialist sector of a healthcare system that often blends into the other two sectors. Folk medicine mixes many different components, though most are related to the popular sector. Some anthropologists divide this sector into sacred and secular, but that distinction blurs in practice.

How are teaching and healing related in Mark? Many different people address Jesus as 'teacher' (Greek *didaskalos;* 4:38; 5:35; 9:17, 38; 10:17, 20, 35; 12:14, 19, 32; 13:1). Jesus uses 'teacher' as a self-identification at least once (14:14). Sometimes this term, as well as the verb 'to teach' *(didaskō),* occurs in a context where a healing takes place (1:21, 22; 2:13; 4:1, 35; 6:2, 6, 30).

The context of these teaching-word occurrences (noun, verb) includes more than healing, but the link with healing occurs too often to be insignificant. Perhaps Mark 9:38 offers a key: "Teacher, another not with us cast out demons." Jesus is addressed as teacher and is questioned about one of the major divisions of the illness taxonomy: demons and unclean spirits. Is Jesus perceived in the folk sector as a teacher-healer?

One way to explore this possibility is to consider Jesus' legitimation or authority to do what he does. In a healthcare system, those with appropriate credentials and authority are considered professionals. Those who lack this legitimation but who engage in healthcare are considered charlatans and quacks in our culture, but folk healers in many other cultures.

In Mark 11:27, the chief priests, scribes, and elders ask Jesus in the Jerusalem temple: "By what authority are you doing these things, or who gave you this authority to do them?" Clearly Jesus does not have legitimacy or publicly recognized official authority; he is not part of the professional sector. On the other hand, in Mark 1:22, the apparently ordinary folk acknowledge that Jesus teaches (in the synagogue) "as one who had authority" and not like the scribes. Though Jesus may not have public official certification, as it were, he does have an authority that is evident in his teaching and healing activity.

Thus, I suggest that Mark presents Jesus as teacher-as-healer, which would classify him in etic terms as a folk healer. Kleinman (1980: 261) notes that the popular image of contemporary Chinese folk healers is that of Confucian scholar. The Confucian paradigm assures that patients do not challenge the treatment style and expect only that secret knowledge, somewhat higher social status, and emotional distance are signs of the healer's therapeutic power. In the case of Jesus, no patient challenged his treatment style. Rather each made some positive judgment about his therapeutic power. For these people, Jesus' powerful teaching revealed a more-than-human legitimation (as the Markan prologue makes clear).

Does it make emic sense to identify Jesus as a teacher/healer in the folk sector of his world? Yes. Jesus and all the people of his culture dealt with sickness as illness and not as disease. Mark's taxonomy clusters illnesses, not diseases. Jesus and all healers of that period could only perceive illnesses, not diseases. Since illness concerns the sociocultural meaning of a sickness experience, it makes good sense to view a teacher as a healer. Notice in each healing instance the almost total disregard of symptoms (something essential to disease). Instead there is constant concern for meaning. The context of Jesus' healing activity is frequently during his teaching activity—in the synagogue, for example. He is engaged in identifying meaning in life, which is the aspect of sickness that medical anthropologists call illness. In this regard, the etic description of Jesus' activity is primarily as healing rather than curing. He provides social meaning for the life problems resulting from the sickness. Actually, we are unable to determine whether Jesus cured anyone since there is no possibility of ascertaining this as the definition of curing requires.

Though biblical persons would not use the etic terminology that this investigation does, it seems probable that they would agree essentially with its conclusions. On the other hand, attempts to identify specific Gospel incidences of unclean spirit or demon activity as incidences of epilepsy, mental illness, and the like, are pseudo-etic interpretations that involve more scientific, Western medicine than an etic interpretation can bear. Ohnuki-Tierney (1981: 32–33) appropriately cautions:

> Although biomedicine may, at least potentially, be viewed as culture-free, the way in which it is practiced is significantly influenced by the values and other cultural factors of a given Western society. . . . Before simplistically equating biomedical categories and clinical processes as etic, we must first do ethnomedical studies of Western medicine so that we come to understand the 'cultural transformations' involved.

CONCLUSIONS

Each healthcare sector speaks a different medical language and holds different sets of beliefs and values in its cognitive structure (Kleinman 1980: 52). It seems possible to begin to draw out these beliefs and values from a social scientific analysis of the text of any biblical author, such as an evangelist.

The reports of the three sectors reflected in a given evangelist would have to make sense to his readership, even if the original events took place in a context whose healthcare beliefs were slightly different. Thus, in Mark (1:29-31) Peter's mother-in-law suffers from a fever, but in Luke (4:38-39) she seems to be possessed by a demon named Fever (Hull 1974: 102–3). In Mark, Jesus lifts her up by the hand, but in Luke he exorcises the demon. While it is possible that Luke is engaging in theological interpretation, medical anthropology regards as axiomatic (based on many studies of many cultures) that even within a single culture, more than one classification structure often exists (Ohnuki-Tierney 1981: 9, 143). Thus, the same event (the illness of Peter's mother-in-law) could have been viewed quite differently by two evangelists and by the respective audiences for whom they wrote. Culture rather than theology guides the interpretation.

The basic definitions listed in the introduction of this chapter raise questions about the insufficiently examined Western biases of Bible interpreters. Many studies of healing in the Bible unquestioningly accept biomedicine as the only legitimate view of reality. From this starting point, such studies seek to examine biblical events in biomedical terms, or explain why the events are or are not possible on the basis of biomedical principles (Kleinman 1980: 57). Yet medical anthropology has discovered that the *materia medica* used in healing is often chosen because of the analogy to the situation or for other culturally symbolic reasons, rather than because of the interaction between the chemical components and a microbe. Still, as anthropologists will point out, their effectiveness is just as real (Ohnuki-Tierney 1981: 48).

Examining Mark with a tripartite model of a healthcare system (popular, professional, and folk sectors) highlights the importance of key cultural factors in the text, such as kinship, social networks, power/authority, and the like. The taxonomy reflected in Mark (event or misfortunes involving spirits or demons, and those not involving spirits or demons) simplifies our understanding of his reports and prepares the way for further analyses that will fit more appropriately into that cultural scheme.

AFTERWORD

By the time I had completed the analysis of Luke's Gospel using the same model as for Mark, colleagues had persuaded me to become skeptical of the taxonomy based on spirit-involvement or no-spirit-involvement. The differing interpretations of the illness of Peter's mother-in-law (in Mark and Matthew, and in Luke) raise doubts. The explanation I offer here in Mark is still valid. It is the larger picture that needs reconsideration. My research in recent years on altered states of consciousness, the resurrection appearances, and the special abilities of the holy person (shamanic healer) in this culture to interact with spirits continues to make me suspect that in the native view, the spirit world is involved in all of human experience whether recognized or not.

Jesus casting out a demon; the calling of Peter
Anonymous engraving, 1491
Staatsbibliothek, Munich, Germany

5

HEALING IN MATTHEW

THE OBSESSION WITH EXHAUSTIVE COMPREHENSIVENESS in biblical research does not necessarily characterize scholarly excellence so much as it reveals different thinking styles (McKenney and Keen 1974: 79–90). Scientific training in biblical exegesis has perhaps emphasized the collection of detail and minutiae at the expense of developing the ability to construct the bigger picture. Individuals who excel at collecting data are often less gifted in creating the larger picture. On the other hand, intuitive thinkers who create the large picture are frequently bored by the pursuit of detail. Obviously, good research will benefit from the blended contribution of all thinking styles (Briggs-Meyers and Meyers 1980).

Biblical data-gatherers can resonate with social scientists who view their methods as "tools of data retrieval" (Ohnuki-Tierney 1981: 9). Yet even when the data is gathered for interpretation, Romanucci-Ross (1978: 135) reminds the investigator that four processes were involved in the project:

I perceive what is going on.
I perceive what is not going on.
I do not perceive what is going on.
I do not perceive what is not going on.

With specific regard to Western scientific methods utilized during her field work in Melanesia, Romanucci-Ross observed that the natives credited Western medicine with "excellent descriptive categories and precise instrumentation but judged it poor in explanatory models: 'What good is your medicine if you can't tell me why I got sick?'" (1969: 119).

In this chapter, we apply to the Gospel of Matthew the same definitions and model applied to Mark in chapter 4. Though it may appear repetitive, the model should help us retrieve either different data from that in Mark or data in a different configuration. My preferred thinking style as a scholar is the intuitive thinking style (Meyers-Briggs type: ENFJ) with a preferred interest in the bigger picture. Detailed investigations of individual healing reports are not the main interest in this volume but will be noted as relevant.

Thus, this chapter is an etic report: It represents an outsider's perspective on a particular insider group's interpretation of reality. The Gospel of Matthew is treated as analogous to a field report (Malina 1983). In other words, the Gospel is an emic document, a native's interpreted report of what is transpiring in that society. Thus the very notion of a healthcare system and its three constitutive sectors (professional, popular, folk) is an etic understanding. People in the first century would not understand this concept but would—if the analysis is carried out correctly—recognize and affirm the judgments made concerning the individuals involved, their perceptions, and their roles in each sector of the system.

Modern Western investigators must suspend their biomedical understandings and assumptions in reading the Gospel. The reality shared by modern individuals and the ancients is good fortune and misfortune, or well-being and lack of well-being. Though this reality may also be called health and lack of health (or sickness), culture begins to intrude to a greater degree in these words. Modern Westerners who accept and live by the principles of biomedicine will call the lack of health "disease" and understand it as a pathological state affecting the individual alone, even if the disease is contagious. In the biomedical perspective the dominant concern is to seek the cause of the disease and the appropriate silver bullet (single remedy) to cure it—that is, to control and/or destroy the pathogens.

The ancients (and many contemporary peoples in traditional societies) view lack of health as illness, that is, as a socially disvalued condition or state that involves and affects many others besides the stricken individual. The primary interest in situations of illness is to identify the symptoms and to find a meaning for them, or to discover how to integrate these symptoms into a meaningful life. That is what healing an illness entails.

In the entire Bible there is no interest at all in disease, since this concept requires awareness of such things as microscopic viruses and bacteria. Such a perspective on the reality called sickness was totally unknown at that time and in that part of the world. Health problems were considered illnesses. It is impolite, inappropriate, and ethnocentrically anachronistic to identify the sicknesses in the Gospel as leprosy, epilepsy, mental illness, in the same sense that these conditions have in modern Western civilization.

THE HEALTHCARE SYSTEM

The etic term, *healthcare system,* covers a broad range of practices such as taking care of the body, beliefs about health maintenance, and formalized as well as non-formalized healthcare treatments. Examples of the latter are health treatments at shrines and treatments by folk healers, by shamans, by exorcists, and so on (Ohnuki-Tierney 1984: 7). For this reason, it is erroneous to consider the healer as the central element in any healing system. The entire system heals, not just the healer. This would suggest that investigations of healing in antiquity or at any time ought to be systemic.

Healing is not simply the outcome of diagnostic acts and interventions. Rather the healing function is active from the very outset in the way the illness is perceived and in the way the experience of illness is organized (Kleinman 1980: 208). A widely accepted model of a healthcare system recognizes three overlapping sectors: professional, popular, and folk (see Figure 2.1). We now turn to this model to guide both the collection and interpretation of the healthcare data reflected in Matthew.

PROFESSIONAL SECTOR

Assuming the Greek word *iatros* to be a relatively reliable reference to a "professional" healer (considering that professions, as they are known and understood in the contemporary world, did not exist in the ancient world; see Freidson 1970), there is only one such reference in Matthew (9:9-13//Mark 2:13-17//Luke 5:27-32). After calling Matthew, Jesus joins him and his colleagues and friends in table fellowship. In response to complaints that he eats with sinners and tax collectors, Jesus in each Gospel cites a popular and familiar proverb: "Those who are well have no need of a physician, but those who are sick" (Matt. 9:12).

Modern physicians would not identify tax collecting or sinning as diseases requiring professional medical treatment. Yet Jesus' application of this proverb about professional healers to sinners and tax-collectors implies that these two classes of people who deviate from social well-being may well exhibit symptoms of an illness. In that cultural milieu, some healer (professional, popular, or folk) might reasonably be expected to address the illness in question.

From this perspective, Matthew's peculiar modification of the tradition is interesting. Only Matthew's Jesus includes Hosea 6:6 in his response to critics: "Go and learn what this means: 'I desire mercy, not sacrifice.'" Mercy, as a Mediterranean value, is the willingness and the actual paying back of debts to God and to other human beings. Sinners are people who fail in interpersonal relationships, and toll-collectors are Judeans in the employ of the ruling power, Rome, to collect tolls from other Judeans, thus failing to be lenient with them in their indebtedness. Matthew's Jesus identifies two categories of needy human beings (sinners and toll-collectors) and contrasts his mercy toward them with the failure of his opponents to show mercy. Jesus' willingness to overlook the interpersonal shortcomings of these Judeans is presented as a healing activity. Perhaps Jesus' mercy will help these people put their social lives in order.

Matthew's Jesus cites Hosea 6:6 again to defend his disciples' plucking corn on the Sabbath (12:7). Their behavior tallies well with Jesus' advice not to be anxious about food, drink, and clothing (6:25-34). The God who feeds the birds surely would not do less for hungry human beings. The owners of the field owe nourishment to the hungry, as it were, on the basis of interpersonal obligations toward other Judeans. The Pharisees would do well to develop similar merciful attitudes. But the Pharisees exhibit no merciful attitude toward Jesus' dealings with tax-collectors and sinners (9:11) nor for the hungry disciples (12:7). Ultimately Jesus rebukes them for their habitual lack of mercy (23:23).

The parable of the unforgiving servant (Matt. 18:21-35) links the showing of mercy with feeling compassion (18:27). Apart from this parable (in which the king is a cipher for God), in Matthew only Jesus shows compassion, as a result of which he heals (9:36; 14:14; 20:34) and feeds (14:14; 15:32) needy people. Luke's Jesus will exhort his disciples to be merciful or show compassion (Luke 6:36).

To summarize, the only likely reference to professional healers by Matthew's Jesus is deliberately nuanced to highlight mercy and compassion as traits that should characterize any healer in every sector. Moreover, if sin and the shortcomings of tax-collecting are implied to be illnesses, the taxonomy of illnesses in Matthew definitely includes more than physical, bodily ills.

THE POPULAR SECTOR

The largest sector of every healthcare system is the popular sector, which embraces the lay, non-professional, and non-specialist. Here people are interested in maintaining well-being. When health status goes awry, this is the sector that first identifies and labels the deviance.

The popular sector contains several overlapping levels: the individual, family, social network, and community beliefs and practices. The modern Western exegete must keep in mind that individuals described in the biblical documents are very different from Western individuals. In the West, the individual is an autonomous, unique person; in the Middle and Far East, a person is always defined in relation to others (Dupont 1980; Ohnuki-Tierney 1984: 67). Such people are dyadic personalities (Malina 1981: 53–60). Their culture is collectivistic in orientation rather than individualistic.

Individual

At the level of dyadic individuals in Matthew, men suffer illnesses that afflict each of the three symbolic zones of the human body (Malina 1981:60–64): heart–eyes (blind 9:27-31; 20:39-44); mouth–ears (mute 9:32-34; 12:22-24) hands–feet (paralytic 8:5-13; 9:1-8; withered hand 12:1-15). The human person is considered to be whole, healthy, complete when all three of these zones function in harmony. If any zone does not function properly, that person is considered to be ill. By restoring the body-part in that malfunctioning zone to full integrity, Jesus heals the person.

In addition, one man is suffering from the repulsive, scaly condition of the skin called "leprosy" in the Bible (8:1-4; see chapter 3), and others are possessed by spirits (8:28-34; 9:32-34; 12:22-24; 17:14-18).

Women in Matthew appear to be afflicted with illnesses that affect the domestic setting, which in the ancient Mediterranean was the sphere proper to women. Fever incapacitates Peter's mother-in-law so she cannot perform the functions of a woman in the household (8:14-15); death weakens a home, the woman's special place, by removing a woman from that setting (9:18-19); the hemorrhaging woman symbolizes domestic power run amok (9:20-22); the possessed daughter (15:21-28), under the power of someone other than male kin, deviates from the norm and thus poses a threat to domestic order and tranquility.

Family and Society

Because biblical/Mediterranean people are dyadic personalities, they operate within social context, primarily kinship settings, including fictive-kin groups. The Judaic official pleads with Jesus on behalf of his deceased daughter (9:18-19); fictive-kin groups bring their needy, like the paralyzed man (9:1-2), to Jesus to be healed. On the other hand, some groups were skeptical of his healing powers. Some of Jesus' kin doubted him (13:57-58); fictive-kin groups challenged him (12:24). Still other groups expelled him from their community (8:34). In the Mediterranean world, groups play a significant role in the healthcare system at the popular level.

Community Beliefs and Practices

A key element governing the behavior of dyadic personalities and the groups in which they are situated is the cluster of beliefs and practices that they hold in common. For instance, Murdock (1980: 58) notes that causation of illness by witchcraft is most characteristic and deep-seated in the circum-Mediterranean region. According to him, witchcraft is the ascription of impairment of health to the suspected voluntary or involuntary aggressive action of a member of a special class of people believed to be endowed with a special power and propensity for evil (21).

Malina and Neyrey (1988) provide the most culturally plausible explanation of this phenomenon in Matthew's Gospel, though they focus more on the process than on the health-related results. Elliott's investigations (1992, 1994) into the Mediterranean evil-eye phenomenon help a careful reader to identify a situation in Matthew in which the potential for serious illness may not have been noticed before. The householder who paid all the day-workers exactly the same wage at the end of the day was given the "evil eye" by those who felt cheated (Matt. 20:15). The immediate expectation, of course, would be that their evil intent was to destroy the harvest or ruin the vineyard. But it could also include a wish for physical harm to the householder himself. The preventive measures against this threat include wearing the color blue, wearing specific talismans, or using specific hand gestures as the threat is made.

Another belief specific to the Matthean community, it would seem, can be observed in that only Matthew (17:14-18; compare 4:24) describes the case of a boy who is "moonstricken" (Ross 1978). Almost all modern exegetes translate and interpret this Greek world to be *epilepsy*. Such a biomedical judgment seems a bit hasty and certainly insensitive to ancient beliefs. The world that Matthew reflects was interested in sickness as a sociocultural phenomenon, that is, as illness. From that perspective, this passage is best investigated—seriously—in the context of the effects of stars and constellations in the sky upon humans on earth, sorcery, evil-eye, witchcraft, spirit-aggression, and other cosmic beliefs that are peculiar to and dominate the circum-Mediterranean area (see chapter 2).

Taxonomy

A more global examination of the illness episodes recounted in Matthew reveals the taxonomy, or division of sicknesses, recognized in Matthew's community. Even if the reports are drawn from earlier traditions, Matthew's presentation of illnesses must fit into the taxonomy familiar and acceptable to his community and his readers. Two sources in which the taxonomy appear to be evident are the healing summaries which occur throughout the Gospel, and the cluster of healings reported in Matthew 8–9.

Summary Reports. Matthew's summary reports of healing (for example, "Jesus healed people who had all kinds of illnesses and maladies": 4:23-24; 7:22; 8:16; 9:35-36; 10:1, 8; 11:5; 12:16; 13:54; 14:14, 35; 15:29-31; 21:14) do not reflect the same dichotomized taxonomy found in Mark's summaries: sicknesses with spirit involvement, and sicknesses with no spirit involvement (see chapter 4).

Among these summary reports, Matthew presents six lists that specify a condition or enumerate a mixture of various illnesses (4:24; 10:8; 11:5; 14:14; 15:29; 21:14) from which it is difficult to deduce any common feature(s). Taxonomies are determined by and reflect the worldview of each society, and this worldview is the source of the common features an investigator seeks in hypothesizing a taxonomy for an ancient society (Ohnuki-Tierney 1984). Expelling demons identifies one illness situation (4:24; 7:22; 8:16; and 10:1, 8). Some of the other listings (4:24; 10:8; 11:5; 15:29-31) present illnesses that reflect one or another of the three symbolic zones of the human body (Malina 1993: 74–81): emotion-fused thought (heart–eyes), self-expressive speech (mouth–ears), and purposeful action (hands–feet). Yet there remain illnesses that do not seem to fit into these or any other category. In other words, if Matthew knows a taxonomy of illnesses, he does not manifest it in his Gospel.

The Cluster of Healing and Other Stories in Matthew 8–9. Of all the illnesses found in Matthew's Gospel, this cluster reports three of the four that affected women: fever, death, and hemorrhage (8:14; 9:18-26); and five of the six that affected men: so-called leprosy (8:1-4), paralysis (8:5-13; 9:1-8), spirit possession (8:28-34; 9:32-34), blindness (9:27-31), and muteness (9:32-34; see also 12:22-24). Matthew's inclusion of Jesus' stilling the storm in this cluster (8:23-27) suggests that healing activity extends beyond physical, bodily ailments and include other misfortunes of which illness is but one example. The taxonomy suggested by the cluster of ten stories in Matthew 8–9 seems to be based on the causes of illness. George Foster (1976: 775) described such taxonomies as naturalistic (natural forces cause illness—for example, blindness) and personalistic (human, non-human, or supernatural agents cause illness—for example, the Gadarene demoniac, the mute demoniac). Romanucci-Ross (1969: 201–9) proposed a different kind of taxonomy: socio-moral (emphasizing a cause explained by cultural norms or native viewpoints—for example, so-called leprosy) and secular-somatic (drawn from the biomedical field—for example, death or near death). Neither of these etic perspectives is entirely successful.

Trying to grasp the emic viewpoint, one notices that of healings in Matthew 8–9 all bear relationship to boundaries. So-called leprosy (see chapter 3) is really a condition like a rash or flakiness that afflicts the skin, the boundary of the human body. Spirit-possession is an invasion and penetration of the person's boundary from without. Paralysis, blindness, and muteness affect one or more of the three symbolic zones that constitute the human body, and even though it is external, the problem suggests that something is awry within the human body. The zones are misaligned, the body deviates from the normal human body, and there is trouble "within" the boundaries. Such a division of illnesses into those caused from without and those caused from within are common in the popular sector (Kleinman 1980: 199).

Moreover, if one accepts the domestic definition of women's illnesses in this cluster, then they also reflect a concern for secure boundaries. Within the home-boundary, the woman's proper sphere of power, one woman dies, that is, she will be removed from the community, and another is incapacitated by fever. Outside the home setting, a space in which women are permitted to travel, one woman suffers from irregular menstrual bleeding, that is, feminine power run amok and definitely out of place in the public arena. This latter condition poses a serious threat to domestic peace and tranquility.

Ohnuki-Tierney (1981: 62) observes that illness taxonomies are determined by a society's worldview. The claim that Matthew's community would have recognized a division of illnesses based on boundaries can be supported on two counts. First, Douglas (1966: 113; Pilch 1981) has convincingly demonstrated that human concerns about body boundaries (skin and orifices) replicate concerns about social boundaries and vice versa. Second, T. R. Hobbs has observed that in 2 Kings, each time Israel is attacked by outside hostile forces, the king suffers some form of a skin problem.

Finally, both Foster (1976: 776) and Worsley (1982: 327) point out that illness is but a special instance of misfortune. Jesus' stilling the storm indicates that healing power touches all misfortune that threatens or plagues human life in the Matthean community. Therefore, Jesus not only heals bodily ills, but also stills storms, feeds hungry crowds, has compassion on harassed crowds, etc.

This taxonomy of illnesses based on boundaries also explains Matthew's summary statements. His generic references to "illnesses and maladies" include a Greek word that only Matthew among the Evangelists uses: *malakia* (4:23; 9:35; 10:1) meaning softness, delicacy, and effeminacy. In the context of concern for boundaries, this word would take on the meaning of 'vulnerable' or 'already penetrated.' Reflections inspired by Mary Douglas (see chapter 3 above, pp. 55ff) on the human body as a symbolic reality that bridges the personal world with the sociocultural world prompt further consideration of Matthew's concern with boundaries. People who are not like John the Baptist wear "soft" garments; that is, they increase the vulnerability of the skin by wearing vulnerable rather than protective clothing. If the human body is a symbolic reality, then such people increase the vulnerability or penetrability of their social body. Vulnerability to boundary penetration or violation of the social body, therefore, would be a specific category of illness Jesus healed. From this perspective, tax-collectors and sinners represent segments of the social body 'already penetrated' who in turn become boundary violators. Tax collectors cooperate with and work for the ruling, foreign power. Not only are they 'already penetrated' by that power, but they also penetrate God's holy community by extending foreign domination even further. Sinners (those who separate themselves or are separated from God and God's community) are also 'already penetrated' by a force hostile to God. Their continued presence in the holy community renders it vulnerable as well. Both need the assistance of a healer, that is, someone who can restore meaning to life.

On a purely physical level, the boundaries of the human body are also vulnerable to penetration, particularly the anal and female genital orifices. The ancient Israelite world was concerned about the appropriate partners who could penetrate females (Lev. 18:16-21). It was shameful for a male to be penetrated by another male (Lev. 18:22). Recent research contributes a fresh understanding of the reasons for prohibiting or fearing a male being penetrated by another male.

Paul Veyne (1988: 76–78) points out that in pagan antiquity, one key factor in homophily was considerations of activity and passivity. Honorable males were expected to be active partners in a relationship. Passivity for a male was shameful. Romans labeled as *impudicus* a free-born and adult male who was a passive sexual partner with another male. Slaves were expected to adopt the passive posture, hence were acceptable partners. Thus, this society did not spend its time wondering whether or not a person was a homosexual. Such people existed in its midst. This society did, however, pay enormous attention to the minutest details of attire, pronunciation, gestures, manner of walking, in order to censure those who demonstrated a lack of *manliness,* whatever might be their sexual tastes or preferences. Manliness is also a concern in the Bible (see Pilch 1993).

Within the context of discussing boundaries and boundary penetration of great concern in Matthew's gospel, then, it is advisable to take a closer look at the *malak-* semantic field in Greek. Louw and Nida (1988: (2) 88.281 list *malakos* in the semantic domain of moral and ethical qualities.

This noun describes the passive male partner in homosexual intercourse. Thus among those who will not inherit the kingdom of God Paul includes "homosexuals" (1 Cor. 6:9). This one English word is the RSV translation of two Greek words: *malakos* and *arsenokoites*. Louw and Nida suggest that it plausible to interpret *malakos* as the passive male and *arsenokoites* as the active male partner in homosexual intercourse. Used alone in classical Greek, *malakos* describes catamites: men and boys used sexually in a passive way. The English rendition in such instances is soft or effeminate.

Malina argues along similar lines that passivity is one concern that lies at the heart of the Bible's various assessments of homosexual behavior. The particular dimension of passivity that is shameful is a man being penetrated by another man. As Malina notes, "Males are to be active, dominant, penetrators, and in control, while females are to be passive, subordinate, penetrated, and controlled. Just as honor and shame are replicated in male and female sexual organs, so too are male and female gender roles replicated in sexual roles: penetrator, penetrated."

Matthew's concerns about boundaries and boundary integrity in chapters 8–9, which include concern for the body's boundaries (lepers in 8:1-4; food in 9:14-17; etc) and bodily integrity suggest an alternate translation of his Greek phrase (*nosos kai malakia;* 4:23; 9:35; 10:1), usually rendered as 'disease and infirmity.' In line with definitions from medical anthropology, I have suggested an alternative rendition 'sickness and illness.' Since illness is concerned with meaning in life, and meaning derives from the social system, from culture, Matthew might be specifying a certain area of Israelite where meaning has been confused and lost. In the Israelite community, the sexual behavior of some males did not reflect the culture's accepted meaning in life. Jesus and his followers therefore healed or restored proper meaning in life to situations of "sickness and effeminacy, that is, male passivity, especially in sexual behavior."

Such a translation resolves the difficulty of distinguishing the two Greek words as two distinct physical conditions. Moreover it resonates with Paul's estimate of shameful and culturally disapproved sexual behaviors (Rom. 1:24-28; see Pilch 1982: 32–33). 'Culturally disapproved' translates a Greek phrase *(para physin)* ordinarily translated 'unnatural,' or 'against nature.' That these translations are inappropriate becomes apparent when the phrase is used again to describe long hair on a man (1 Cor. 11:14) or in the metaphor explaining how non-Israelites fit in as members of the Israelite community (Rom 11:24).

FOLK SECTOR

Matthew uses the Greek word *seleniazesthai* (4:24; 17:15) to describe (presumably) the same illness the other evangelists identify as a case of spirit-possession (Mark 9:14-29//Luke 9:37-43a). Since only Matthew uses this word at all in the Gospels, this may be a clue to Jesus' identity as a folk healer. The word literally means 'moonstruck,' and reflects the community belief that human beings could be affected for good or ill by stars, constellations, planets, and the sun and moon. The psalmist is confident the Lord protects from all adversity: "The sun shall not smite you by day, nor the moon by night" (Ps. 121:6). That Matthew alone uses this word to describe an illness Jesus heals might reflect his community's preference to view Jesus not so much as an exorcist but as a folk healer who can deal with the results of the broad area that includes the effects of the environment as well as the activity known as witchcraft.

The fact that not all those who recognized his power considered it to be legitimate (12:24; 21:23) would strengthen this identification, for the folk sector of any healthcare system is the non-professional and non-bureaucratic sector of that system. It mixes many components from the other sectors, but most of its components are derived from and related to the popular sector. Arguments about the source of Jesus' power—Beelzebul, or the spirit of God (12:27-28; 13:53-58)—add further strength to the suggestion that Jesus is viewed as a folk healer (a folk healer's power is judged as real and effective but is not accepted by everyone as legitimate). Moreover, the argument recognizes that Jesus' power is an intrinsic attribute and not an acquired skill. This is the basis on which witchcraft accusations could legitimately be leveled at Jesus (Murdock 1980: 67; see Malina and Neyrey 1988: 2–32).

It would seem that the folk sector of Mark's community viewed Jesus as a teacher-healer (See chapter 4). The folk sector of Matthew's community does not share this view of Jesus. Scholars note that competing groups contemporary with Jesus differed about the source of his healing power. Moreover, his enemies evaluated his power negatively. Both these factors serve as additional signs of witchcraft accusations (Pamment 1981; Malina and Neyrey 1988).

This is not to say that anyone—modern or ancient—thought that Jesus was a witch. According to Murdock (1980: 68), even though witchcraft is widespread in the circum-Mediterranean area and associated particularly with the evil eye, it is generally presumed to *cause* illness and practically never reported as contributing in any way to its healing. No one ever accused Jesus of causing illness. Precisely what kind of folk healer Jesus was perceived to be in Matthew's community is not yet entirely clear, but a more specific identification may well emerge from additional research along the lines of witchcraft accusations and the evil eye.

CONCLUSION

In Malina's group and grid scheme, the Matthean community would be strong group and low grid (1986; see also White 1986). This kind of community believes in good and effective therapy that is routinely frustrated by the wrong moral attitudes of healer and client. In two instances unique to Matthew (8:13 and 9:27), Jesus places special emphasis on the faith of the petitioner. Where faith was lacking, the disciples feared the storm (8:26), Jesus' healing power was largely ineffective in unbelieving Nazareth (13:58), and Jesus scolded his generation as faithless (17:17) and said his disciples had little faith (17:20). Recall that faith in the Mediterranean world is best understood as loyalty, in this case, unswerving loyalty to God and to Jesus, the broker of healing from God.

In addition, a strong group and low grid community searches out responsibility for the misfortune chiefly in order to delineate, explicitly and plainly, covert factional lines. Thus witchcraft accusations are a normal challenge to existing authority. From such a perspective, denying or questioning Jesus' legitimate authority to heal is a tacit acknowledgment of it and of its true source in a real sense.

AFTERWORD

In revising this chapter, I became more fully aware of the etic nature of the illness taxonomies I was proposing for Matthew (as I had for Mark). Recall that the etic perspective is that of an outsider. The investigator works from a culture different from the one under investigation. The etic perspective, therefore, will almost always fall short in the beginning. For this reason it is an imposed etic perspective. Eventually in a process of mutual refinement of both perspectives (etic and emic), points of comparison might appear, and then the researcher will have attained a derived etic perspective that will facilitate cross-cultural comparisons and interpretation (Pilch 1996a).

Jesus healing the paralytic man
Julius Schnorr von Carolsfeld

6

HEALING IN LUKE–ACTS

SICKNESS AND HEALING, while common features in Luke–Acts, are by no means easy to understand. Let us take, for example, the number of times that blindness and its healing occur in Luke's two volumes. The evangelist narrates the traditional story of how Jesus healed a blind man (Luke 18:35-43// Matt. 9:27-51// Matt. 20:29-34// Mark 10:46-52). In Acts, however, we have the curious phenomenon of the temporary blindness of Paul from which he is quickly healed (9:18; 22:13). Along with this, we find the story of Paul cursing Elymas, the magician, with blindness; this blindness, says Paul, is due to "the hand of the Lord" and will last "for a time" (13:6-11). Blindness, then, may be either longstanding, perhaps signaling a genuine disease, or temporary, as in the case of Paul and Elymas. Blindness happened to Paul, who was a sinner (Gal. 1:13; 1 Cor. 15:9), and Elymas, who opposed the gospel, thus suggesting a symbolic dimension to it. Yet how are we to understand these varying examples of sickness and healing? The issue is: How do we understand these accounts? What is an adequate, that is, culturally plausible scenario for understanding this and similar material in Luke–Acts?

Readers are too often misled by the assumption that Luke, the author of Luke–Acts, is the same "Luke the physician" whom Paul greets in Col. 4:14. And so they explore the nature of physical blindness, contrasting real blindness with metaphorical blindness and investigating spontaneous healing and other similar avenues of interpretation. This is the result of our modern, scientific perspective, which has been called medical materialism (Pfifferling 1981; Kleinman 1980).

Even modern attempts to respect the meanings of the Greek and Hebrew vocabulary of the Bible that describe these sickness and healing events encounter a formidable problem. One scholar (Hemer 1986: 52) correctly cautions: "It is important to see words in terms of usage, not to argue from theoretical studies of etymologies, and so to realize the inherent flexibility of language, whose nuances are not to be hardened into subtly rigid distinctions of general application."

Thus on the basis of his varied Greek vocabulary alone (*nosoi, mastigoi, astheneia,* etc.) very little if anything can be safely deduced about Luke's understanding of sickness and healing. A new perspective is needed. It is important to name the obstacles that a modern reader faces in trying to read Luke's healing stories. But naming the problems is not enough.

If the problem of interpretation lies in our perception, how can we adjust our viewpoint to perceive things like Luke did? What is needed is a way to imagine Luke's language of sickness and healing in terms of his own culture. It is imperative to design a new scenario (Malina 1996a). Sensitivity to cultural differences and the requirements of cross-cultural investigations and comparisons call for the reader to utilize appropriate social-scientific methods and concepts. How different, but how necessary, it is for us to understand that health or well-being is but an example of *good fortune* (Worsley 1982: 330). Alternately, sickness is but one example of a wide range of *misfortunes.* The key lies in understanding the relation of sickness and healing to fortune and misfortune—not a very modern idea, but one quite frequent in, and more appropriate to, other cultures.

To understand why a specific sickness is considered a misfortune in a given society, one needs also to know the cultural values and social norms of that society. Let us try, then, to see sickness and healing from the cultural perspective of Luke, who was certainly not a physician, in modern, scientific terms, and very likely not a physician as defined in antiquity either.

Social-scientific methods and concepts are tools of retrieval as well as aids to interpretation (see chapter 5 and Pilch 1986). This chapter, then, calls upon and constructs several social-scientific models for reading the stories about illness and healing in Luke–Acts: (1) cross-cultural concepts of sickness and healing, (2) the healthcare system in Luke–Acts, (3) a taxonomy of illnesses, and (4) a focus on blindness as central in the storyline of Luke–Acts. In the light of cross-culturally appropriate methods, models, and concepts, many hitherto undetected data in Luke–Acts emerge as significant.

The application of cross-culturally developed methods, models, and concepts regarding healthcare systems helps cast Jesus' and his followers' healing activity in a new light. This approach, moreover, serves as a useful check against the ethnocentric bias or theological creativity of an investigator. Furthermore, the taxonomy or way of clustering the healings of Jesus reported in Luke–Acts should reflect the values that guide one *Mediterranean* way of perceiving and interpreting health realities.

When all is said and done, we shall return to the issue of blindness and healing mentioned at the opening of this chapter. Blindness is a key theme in Luke–Acts, which this chapter will situate in the context of the social-scientific models about to be developed. It is our hope that we can then demonstrate that Luke's distinctive presentation of Jesus as healer of blindness makes a specific appeal to his audience.

DEFINING HEALTH AND HEALING IN LUKE–ACTS

How hard—but how necessary—it is for us to learn the lesson that "It is no longer possible to assume that generalizations based on observations of one culture have a universal applicability" (Papajohn and Spiegel 1975: 19). Bible interpreters need to be wary of imposing observations drawn from Western culture upon Mediterranean culture. Scientifically based Western understandings of health and sickness, sight and blindness, and healing and curing cannot be imposed upon information from the biblical period. Medical anthropology identifies this erroneous methodology as *medicocentrism:* a belief that scientific Western medicine is the only truth relative to health and sickness questions; that outside this framework there is no truth, and it is highly doubtful any authentic cures may take place; and that apparent cures can be explained by subsequent advances in scientific knowledge or perhaps as a form of mind-over-matter. The appropriate scenario rejects medicocentrism for understanding sickness and healing, choosing instead to deal dramatically with the issue posed by a culture foreign to ours.

I explained this model for comparing values across culture in chapter 1, in which I applied it to mainstream U.S. culture and Mediterranean culture. Illustrations of Mediterranean culture were drawn from Luke–Acts. The model contributed to the coining of two different definitions of healing, one appropriate to each of the cultures reviewed, based on the contrasting value preferences of each culture. This first model on viewpoint and value, then, has gone far toward equipping a reader of Luke–Acts with the tools for understanding sickness and healing in that different culture. To review, the emphasis one would expect in Luke–Acts would be as follows:

1. on being and/or becoming (that is, on states), not on doing (activity)
2. on collateral and linear relationships, not on individualism
3. on present and past time orientation, not on the future
4. on the uncontrollable factor of nature, not on its manipulation or mastery
5. on human nature, which can be both good and bad, not neutral or correctable

This viewpoint and the values it embodies would yield a definition of health as a state of complete well-being, not the restoration of individual activity or performance as the values of the Western world, in general, would require. Sickness and healing, then, would be perceived quite differently in this matrix compared to our Western, scientific perspective. Different values are at stake.

This model in chapter 1 has given us a general viewpoint and a broad horizon against which to read Luke's two-volume work. The generality of this first step requires that we move closer to the documents and examine them in greater detail to learn the specific ways in which Luke speaks of sickness and healing, that is a Lukan taxonomy of illness. But to put that into proper context, we next need to present some basic definitions and to present the healthcare system that is reflected in Luke–Acts.

THE HEALTHCARE SYSTEM IN LUKE–ACTS

As we begin to examine specific passages in Luke–Acts, we must be as clear as possible on the terms we use to describe and classify the sickness mentioned there. Fortunately, we are not the first readers to grapple with this problem; we can borrow the standard terms used by the field of medical anthropology. In this way, we can tap into the valuable work done there, even as we gain a necessary precision in our professional language.

In medical anthropology, the word *sickness* is considered a blanket term describing a reality, while the words *disease* and *illness* are considered explanatory concepts and terms useful in exploring different facets of that single reality. Think of sickness as genus, and disease and illness as species. It is important to note that these English words have been so designated in modern times by medical anthropologists to describe more accurately the human experience of misfortune in the realm of health and well-being. These words do not seem to have any one-to-one counterpart in classical or New Testament Greek. In other words, Greek or Hebrew words that are translated 'disease' or 'illness' or even 'sickness' in the Bible reflect the interpretation of the translator and should not be interpreted with the medical anthropological precision just indicated. In this regard Hemer's caution about drawing conclusions based on the "uncertain terminology of literary sources" such as New Testament Greek vocabulary is quite appropriate. The modern interpreter needs to ask of each instance in the biblical literature: Can this emic (native) report be fairly interpreted by the etic (outsider, in this case medical anthropological) term *disease* or *illness?* (On this problem, still largely unrecognized by exegetes, see my comments in chapter 4, pp. 57–58).

DISEASE

The concept and word *disease* reflect a biomedical perspective that sees abnormalities in the structure or function of organ systems. Whether or not they are culturally recognized, these pathological states do exist (Kleinman 1980: 72). As such, a disease affects individuals and only individuals are treated. To think in terms of individuals and individual disease is a perspective quite foreign to Luke's first-century world, which was radically group oriented, as we noted in previous chapters. In such a world, persons were collectivistic personalities, dyadic individuals rather than rugged individualists (Malina 1993: 63–89).

Considering that this kind of knowledge of disease hinges on the identification of pathogens, germs, viruses, and other microscopic entities, it is clear that biblical people would be entirely ignorant of a disease. They might be experiencing one but would not have the necessary concepts or terminology to know and express it. Evidently, if we are interested in Luke's narrative and his cultural world, we will not use the term *disease* very much if at all, for it is a term foreign to Luke' culture. Instead, we will employ the term *illness*.

ILLNESS

The concept and word *illness* reflect a sociocultural perspective that depends entirely upon social and personal perception of certain socially disvalued states including, but not necessarily restricted to, what modern Western science would recognize as a disease. Let us cite a classic example. Leprosy as described in the Lev. 13–14 is simply not the modern Hansen's Disease *(mycobacterium leprae),* but rather some kind of repulsive skin condition. Yet the sociocultural concern over, and consequences of, this condition are very real. In other words, biblical leprosy is definitely not a disease but an illness (see chapter 3).

CURING AND HEALING

Technically speaking, when therapy can affect a disease so as to check or remove it, that activity is called *curing*. As a matter of actual fact, cures are relatively rare even in modern, Western scientific medicine. When an intervention affects an illness, that activity is called *healing*. The rule of thumb is: curing is to disease as healing is to illness. Since healing essentially involves the provision of personal and social meaning for the life problems that accompany human health misfortunes, all illnesses are always and infallibly healed, since all human beings ultimately find some meaning in a life-situation, including disvalued states.

In biblical reports evidence for the incidence, identification, and management of disease is difficult if not impossible to discover with certitude. Thus it cannot be known with certainty whether in modern terms anyone ever cured an afflicted person. And so, modern readers of the Gospels might be taking a hopeless and even misguided approach if they concentrate on issues of 'disease' and 'curing.' On the other hand, in modern terminology the obvious social concern that accompanies the reports of human health-related misfortunes in the New Testament is evidence that the discussion of them in the Gospels centers on 'illness,' and these are almost always 'healed.' This suggests that all of Jesus' dealings with the sick in Luke's Gospel are truly healings, although they may not be cures in the technical sense.

THE HEALTHCARE SYSTEM

Although no one is quite sure whether healthcare now or ever was delivered in a systematic fashion (Mackintosh 1978), the healthcare system is a conceptual model with three constituent and overlapping parts: a professional sector, a popular sector, and a folk sector (see Figure 2.1, p. 26). Actually, it would be more accurate to call this a sickness care system since that is the primary focus, but *health*care system is the recognized term and it is a good heuristic tool for analyzing the way sickness in all cultures is identified, labeled (that is, placed into a taxonomy or proper category), and managed.

THE PROFESSIONAL SECTOR

The professional sector of a healthcare system includes the professional, trained, and credentialed healers. If the Greek word *iatros* (usually translated as "physician") can be assumed to identify a professional healer, there are two (possibly three) relevant passages to review: Luke 4:23; 5:31; and 8:43.

1. The proverb Jesus cites in 4:23, "'Physician, heal yourself'; what we have heard you did at Capernaum, do here also in your own country," is common to the Synoptics and common in antiquity (Noland 1979). It always depends on context for its meaning, and the word *physician* is almost always applied figuratively. An analogous modern proverb, Every dog has its day, almost never refers to dogs, but humans are never offended when this proverb is applied to situations of human misfortune or bad luck.

The Lukan context (4:21-44) is larger than that found in the other evangelists. It suggests that Jesus identifies himself as a prophet (4:24) who exorcises and heals. The identity is repeated and confirmed in 13:33: "I cast out demons and perform healings. . . . It cannot be that a prophet should perish away from Jerusalem." Others acknowledge and reinforce the identity, too (Luke 7:16; 9:8, 19; 24:19). Being a prophet who exorcises and heals is very likely part of Jesus' specific identity as a folk healer.

2. In 5:31, Luke's Jesus once more quotes a proverb: "Those who are well have no need of a physician, but those who are sick." It is cited as an explanation for his associating with tax-collectors and sinners. Only in Luke does Jesus specify that he has come to call sinners "to repentance" *(eis metanoian)*.

Once again the context of the word *physician* adds a further piece of information useful for understanding the kind of illness a healer in Luke's community would be expected to address. Tax-collecting and the condition of a sinner entailed a distortion of social life as it should properly be lived in Israel. To refocus one's personal meaning in life, repentance/*metanoia* is required. That, in fact, is a consistent subject of preaching (see Luke 3:3, 8; 5:2; 10:13; 11:32; 13:3, 5; 15:7, 10; 16:30; 17:3, 4; 24:27; Acts 2:38; 3:19; 8:22; 11:18; 13:24; 17:30; 19:4; 20:21; 26:20).

3. Though omitted in important manuscripts (P[75], B, D), Luke 8:43 (//Mark 6:26) is found with a variant lection in others (א, A, C, K, L, P, W): "and (the woman who suffered from a flow of blood for twelve years) had spent all her living upon physicians." On the basis of manuscript evidence and customary Lukan style, it makes sense to omit the phrase. That Luke, the alleged physician, deliberately struck it from his source to spare "his own" from criticism is an unwarranted anachronistic interpretation. His Gospel exhibits the kind of healthcare knowledge that every educated person would know; it contains no information that only a physician would know or report.

From a medical anthropological perspective, Mark, who underscores the failure of physicians to heal the woman, highlights the failure of the professional sector of the healthcare system in this instance. Luke, whether or not he has willfully expunged the criticism of physicians, quite clearly points to the failure of *all* sectors of the healthcare system in the phrase he does use: she "could not be healed by anyone."

Further, by mentioning physicians explicitly, Mark (and perhaps also Luke?) would be specifying the sector in which the woman might have placed the most confidence, considering that this is where her resources were exhausted. Folk healers, after all, are not entirely free either (Press 1982: 192–93). In the ancient Mediterranean world, a person involved in a healing transaction with anyone would be involved in a dyadic contract and would definitely owe the healer something. In the Gospels, rather than pay Jesus directly, people give glory to God (for example, 7:16; Malina 1993: 99). In summary, neither in the Gospel nor Acts is there any direct and explicit information about the professional sector of the healthcare system. Yet the key word that belongs to that sector offers insight into the community's understanding of the role of a healer and the nature of illness.

In the Gospel, Jesus adopts the image of a healing prophet, or prophet-healer. A central function of his healing ministry is to lead those whose lives have lost cultural meaning back to the proper purpose and direction in life. That is, the prophet-healer preaches repentance, change of heart, transformation of horizons, broadening of perspectives.

The Popular Sector

The principal concern of the lay, non-professional, non-specialist popular culture is health and health maintenance, not sickness and cure. But obviously this focus on health sensitizes people to notice deviance from the culturally defined norm known as health. Therefore, it is in this, the popular sector, that the deviant condition known as sickness is first observed, defined, and treated. There are several levels in the popular sector of the healthcare system: the individual, family, social network, and community beliefs and activities. Each level yields additional information about the entire system.

Individual

At the level of individual dyadic persons, Luke–Acts reports twenty-three cases involving men and eight involving women. In the Gospel, men are afflicted in three symbolic body zones (Malina 1979, 1993; more on the meaning of this in a subsequent section): mouth–ears (1:20, 64; 11:14-23; 22:47-54a); hands–feet (5:17-26; 6:6-11); heart–eyes (7:21; 18:35-43). People with skin problems (lepers; see chapter 3) are cleansed (5:12-16; 17:11-19). Possessed individuals are freed (4:31-37; 8:26-34; 9:37-43a; 11:14-23). And the dead or near dead are raised (7:1-10, 11-16). The cases in Acts involving men reflect only two of the symbolic three body zones: hands–feet (3:1-10; 9:32-35; 14:8-18; 28:1-6) and heart–eyes (9:18 //22:13; 13:1-12). Spirit-induced ills afflict Herod (12:13, stricken by an angel of the Lord, eaten by worms) and the sons of Sceva (19:14-16). There is one raising from the dead (20:7-12).

Women in the Gospel reflect distinctively feminine experiences, such as difficulty in conception (1:24; 1:35) and menstrual irregularity (8:42b-48). One is raised from the dead (8:40-42a, 49-56), one released from a fever (4:38-39), one is freed from a spirit of infirmity (13:10-17) and others from evil spirits (8:2). In Acts only two cases involving women are reported: Tabitha is raised from the dead (9:36-43), and a slave girl is released from bondage to an evil spirit (16:16-24).

At this point, what does the healthcare system model reveal? Men and women are reported to suffer a variety of ills, some of which are experienced by both groups (death; possession of a spirit) and others by each group singly: only men are reported with skin problems/leprosy, only women suffer from difficulty in conception and menstrual irregularity, distinctively female problems

Further, only men's ills seem to fit into one of the three identified symbolic body zones, though it is possible that women's ailments seem mainly to effect the zone of hands–feet, that is, purposeful activity. Curiously, in the Gospel all three zones are affected, while in Acts only two are affected. We shall need another model to interpret the significance of this observation; it will be presented and explained below in the discussions of taxonomies of illness. What emerges from a bird's-eye view of Luke–Acts at this level of the healthcare system model is that specifically feminine ailments of the Gospels no longer plague women in Acts, though—as with the men—evil/unclean spirits still pose problems, as also does death. We shall return to this consideration below in the fuller discussion of the three symbolic body zone model.

Family

Kinship is one of the two formal institutions in the ancient Mediterranean world, so it is no surprise that the family—including fictive kin—is involved and affected in many of the instances reported in Luke–Acts. For instance, the death of a son is tragic enough, but for a widow it is double jeopardy (7:11-16) since she relies on that male next-of-kin for her very livelihood. Jesus effectively saved *her* life by restoring her son to *his* life. Conversely, when Paul healed the slave girl with the spirit of divination (Acts 16:24), her masters felt adversely affected by her good fortune. In all cultures, no sick person suffers alone; kin and fictive kin are always affected and involved in all the stages of the illness.

This level of the healthcare system model reminds the investigator that in the Mediterranean world, even more so than in the modern Western world, illness affects and involves everyone in the kinship group. The consequences of healings therefore affect this wider group as well.

Social Network

Still another pathway for seeking help in an illness episode is the social network, that is, the set of contacts—relatives, friends, neighbors—through which individuals maintain a social identity; receive emotional support, material aid, services, and information; and develop new social contacts (Mitchell 1969; Weidman 1982).

One way that health status is maintained and continually checked among the personalities who populate the pages of the Bible follows the normal pattern of dyadic relationships. Malina (1979; 1993: 63–89) notes that in the Middle East, persons are not viewed as individuals but rather as dyadic personalities; the same is true in the Far East (Ohnuki-Tierney 1984: 67; Dumont 1980). Such persons live in a continual dependence upon the opinions of others, including the judgment of whether or not one is ill.

Berkman classifies networks into two major categories: according to structure or morphology, or according to the type or quality of interaction. For example, consider Peter's and John's healing of the paralytic beggar in Acts 3:1–4:22. The paralytic was carried to the temple gate daily by "them," probably family, friends, or neighbors. Crippled from birth and more than 40 years old, he was known by many, some of whom may have been daily benefactors. Thus, in the crippled man's network, those who carried him maintained one kind or quality of interaction, probably rooted in *ḥesed* (solidarity, a kinship virtue), whereas those who saw him begging and gave alms had another quality of interaction with him, probably rooted in *ṣedekah* (righteousness) (Isa. 56:1; Sir. 3:29—4:10).

Community Beliefs and Practices

Finally, the popular sector of the healthcare system is characterized by a distinctive set of community beliefs and practices (Gaines 1982: 243–44). For example, belief in spirits and spirit-aggression, including possession, is found in all the Gospels but seems especially prominent in Luke. Murdock observes that such a belief is virtually universal and shows no tendency to cluster in a particular ideational region, as do witchcraft theories, for example. Evidence indicates that every society that depends primarily on animal husbandry for its economic livelihood regards spirit-aggression as either the predominant or an important secondary cause of illness. This is especially true where large domestic animals are the focus: camels, cattle, sheep, and goats (Murdock 1980: 73).

Murdock conjectures that this phenomenon might possibly derive from the aleatory (risk) dimension of life, because shepherd-types appear to be at greater risk than land-owner types. Shepherd-types deal with aggression all the time: they must protect themselves and their animals from other people and/or animals, and they must always be prepared to use aggression to ward off aggression. Of course, shepherd-types can also suffer from nature, so they have to depend upon the protection and support of other-than-human beings or persons like spirits who possess some degree of mastery over nature.

As mentioned above, Luke's worldview lies heavily under the influences of spirits, demons, and the like. Jesus is conceived by the power of the holy Spirit (1:35), and at his baptism the Holy Spirit descends upon him in the form of a dove (3:21). Still full of the Holy Spirit and under his impulse, Jesus goes to the desert to do battle with the devil, a malicious spirit whom he bests (4:1-13). Then Jesus returns in the power of the Spirit to Galilee, teaches in synagogues, and one day reads the text of Isaiah that says: "The Spirit of the Lord is upon me." In the very next episodes, while teaching in the Capernaum synagogue, Jesus frees a man from the unclean spirit that had possessed him (4:31-37), then—following the interpretation of Hull (1974)—he frees Simon's mother-in-law from the demon "Fever" that had possessed her (4:38-39). The section ends with a summary statement that Jesus healed people sick with a variety of illnesses and "demons also came out of many" (4:40-41). Finally, in a passage found only in Luke, Jesus asserts: "Behold I cast out demons and perform healings today and tomorrow" (13:32). He thus proclaims his identity as an exorcist. Recall the evidence from the professional sector above, where Jesus is presented as a prophet who heals and exorcises.

In addition to the spirit-related illness episodes reported by other evangelists (Luke 4:33-37; 8:26-39; 9:37-43a, 49; 11:14-15, 24-26), Luke adds these reports: disciples against demons (10:17) ; Satan entered Judas (22:3); Satan wants to sift Simon (22:31-34); Deacon Philip casts out unclean spirits (Acts 8:7); Herod afflicted by angel of the Lord (12:23); Paul's power through handkerchiefs and cloths against evil spirits (19:12), and the sons of Sceva (19:14-16).

In Luke's descriptions of ailments afflicting women, the spirit is also given a prominent place: Peter's mother-in-law is afflicted by a spirit named Fever (4:38); among the women who follow Jesus, some were freed from evil spirits and infirmities (8:2-3); in the raising of Jairus' daughter, Luke notes: "her spirit returned and she got up at once" (8:58); the stooped-over woman had a spirit of infirmity (13:10) and was bound by Satan for eighteen years (13:16); and Paul liberates a woman possessed by a spirit of divination (Acts 16:16).

In summary, it should be obvious that in Luke's understanding and reports, spirit-possession looms very large, and healers such as Jesus, Peter, Philip the deacon, and Paul must be able to address this human ailment with some measure of success. Furthermore, the four levels operative in the popular sector of the healthcare system bring to the surface much information about illness (including the results of spirit-aggression) in the world of Luke–Acts, as well as those who are afflicted by and involved with the illness (men and women; families; and social networks). The heuristic value of this part of the model seems apparent, but its inability to interpret all the information surfaced makes the investigator impatient to move on to another model, taxonomies of illness. Yet one more sector of the healthcare system model, the folk sector, awaits exploration before we can make that move.

The Folk Sector

In Luke's Gospel, Jesus identifies himself as an authorized, spirit-filled prophet who vanquishes unclean spirits and the illnesses associated with them. His constituency accepts and affirms this identity (Luke 7:16; 9:8, 19; 14:19). In addition, Jesus heals illnesses not associated with any spirit. As such, then, Luke's Jesus is a folk healer, and his "license to practice" is tacitly granted and acknowledged by each individual sick person and the local community. Luke's report that some of the crowd (Matthew specifies that it was the Pharisees) doubted his abilities as a folk healer and questioned the source of his power (Luke 11:15//Matt. 9:34) only highlights the limitations of a folk healer's abilities. Indeed, some communities prefer that the folk healer not practice in their midst (see Luke 8:37).

The power of Jesus relative to evil spirits and demons, however, is noteworthy. Except for exorcisms, Jesus generally has no power at all in his social world (Malina 1986: 83). Power is the capacity to produce conformity based on what is necessary for the good of the group. And politics deals in part with how members of a group achieve and use power to implement public goals (Lewellen 1983: 89). Jesus' exorcisms, the instances in which he does have access to power, can be identified from the definition of politics just given as political actions performed for the purpose of restoring correct order to society. Since kinship and politics were the only two formal—that is, distinct and free-standing—social institutions that existed in the first-century Mediterranean world, the political dimensions of Jesus' healing activity would be self-evident to all witnesses, friendly and hostile alike.

Contemporary medical anthropology supports this insight. It views a theory of disease as a sign or emblem that marks what a group values, disvalues, and preoccupies itself with (Fabrega 1974: 274). In Jesus' world, spirit-possession was certainly a disvalued state, while the relationship of spirits to this world certainly preoccupied him and his contemporaries.

Within this scheme, the healing enterprise is concerned with diagnosing the problem, making a prognosis, and applying suitable therapies. Another way of viewing this process is that the healing enterprise seeks to explain, predict, and control reality. In the Beelzebul episode (Luke 11:14-26), the problem diagnosed is a case of spirit-possession. The prognosis or predicted outcome is that the cast-out spirit might return with seven more powerful demons to repossess the person. The therapy Jesus applied—or the reality Jesus seeks to control—is "he who is not with me is against me, who does not gather with me scatters" (11:23). Since Jesus has effective power against demons, he has the power to maintain order in society as it should be. By keeping demons in their place, Jesus maintains good order in society. He also controls reality as he and his contemporaries understood it. Anyone who would stand in the way of that power, challenge it, or obstruct it, stands in the way of the order that belongs in society.

The healers in Acts (Peter and John, Paul, Ananias, Stephen, and Philip) are presented as continuing the healing activity of Jesus, much like Elisha is deliberately presented by the author of 1 and 2 Kings as continuing the work of his master Elijah (Hobbs 1985). Peter's and John's healing of the crippled man in Acts 3:1—4:22 is an explicit example. Though folk healers in general vary widely from culture to culture and even within a culture, some common characteristics can be observed across cultures (Press 1982).

The folk healer shares significant elements of the constituency's world-view and health concepts. All the Mediterranean contemporaries of Jesus and his followers believed in the reality of a spirit world that regularly med-dled in human affairs. The reason why the spirit world might appear more evident or active in Luke than in the other evangelists is that his readers were very likely more inclined to this way of perceiving and understanding.

Folk healers accept *everything* that is presented (technically described as behavioral and somatic symptoms) as naturally co-occurring elements of a syndrome. The story of the Gerasene demoniac (8:26-33) is a good exam-ple. That he wore no clothes and lived, not in a house, but among tomb-stones are some of the behaviors that a modern Western diagnostician (other than a psychiatrist) would put aside in order to focus on the "real" problem, the "alleged" possession. The folk healer views everything as of equal importance. When Luke reports that the healed demoniac was now "clothed," it is probable that Jesus encouraged him to dress, or at least made it possible for him to acknowledge what he ought to do about his ap-pearance. Likewise, Jesus' final instruction to return home and tell what God did may also be part of the therapy instructing him on his proper res-idence: home, and not among tombstones.

The majority of folk healers treat their clients as outpatients. Amusing or silly as this self-evident statement might sound, it is a key element in the folk-healing process, especially among Mediterranean peasants who are very public people (Hall 1983). Jesus and his healing disciples in Luke–Acts always have a crowd or an audience. It was difficult for Jesus to find an isolated place to rest and pray. The publicity involved in healing episodes is very likely bound up with the core values of Mediterranean culture, honor and shame. The folk healer is an honorable person but needs to enjoy continuing success to maintain honor. A crowd will always assure this honor because it witnesses the successful venture.

Folk healers take the patient's view of illness at face value. In no instance did Jesus ever ignore or correct the presenting symptoms as communicated by the sick person or surrogate. Different cultures tend to emphasize one area of symptoms more than others. Modern Italians favor visceral symptoms in their reports, while the Irish favor throat-area symptoms (Press 1982: 190). The pan-Mediterranean emphasis on the visual dimensions of existence (Gilmore 1982: 197) may explain the prevalence of concerns about blindness and seeing in Luke–Acts.

The folk healer's vocabulary for describing an illness is invariably associated with the sick person's everyday experience and belief system. The varied terms for malevolent spirits (unclean spirits, evil spirits, demons, etc.) quite likely reflect the lay perspective on this kind of illness, which is rooted in the Mediterranean belief in spirits. Contemporary Western exegetes who seek to tally and distinguish the various kinds of spirits mentioned are likely expecting too much precision from the first-century Mediterranean vocabulary.

Since folk healers are native to the community and know well its mores, history, and scandals, they make special use of the historical and social context of each illness. Jesus taught in the synagogue-community centers (Luke 4:15; see McKay 1992); many of his healings took place in that context or bore some relationship to the synagogue (Luke 4:33; 6:6; 7:1—the centurion built the synagogue; 8:40—Jairus, chief of the synagogue; 13:10). Through the social network of the synagogue and its informal communication system, the personal lives of those who attend would be known and disseminated. While the Gospel narratives often sound as if petitioners meet Jesus for the first time, it is highly probable that his visits and teaching activity in the various synagogues provided him with more than a passing acquaintance with many people in the area. They may even have been members of a far-flung personal kinship network involving actual and fictive kin of Jesus himself.

In conclusion, Luke's portrayal of Jesus as an anointed, spirit-filled, exorcising-and-healing prophet, and the community's general acknowledgment and acceptance of him as such, sets Jesus clearly in the folk sector of the healthcare system reflected in Luke–Acts. The summary statements in

Luke's Gospel repeatedly tell of the people who came to hear him teach, be healed of ills, and be purged of unclean spirits.

Thus, the healthcare system model with its three intersecting sectors not only helps mine more information from the text than a cursory reading, but also describes the context in which healers would function. Insights from the professional and the popular sectors flesh out the picture of Jesus' activity, which is properly situated in the folk sector of that system. It is now time to focus more specifically on the misfortunes Jesus healed and try to build a taxonomy that would best account for those reported in Luke–Acts.

TAXONOMIES OF ILLNESSES IN LUKE–ACTS

The identification, classification, and clustering of illnesses into culturally meaningful categories is called a taxonomy. In the modern, scientific, Western practice of medicine, a very complete taxonomy of physical and mental health problems can be found in exhaustive manuals of differential diagnosis. Your physician may have consulted such a book after listening to your report of a recent physical experience or set of experiences. The modern physician's challenge is to translate your "lay" report into appropriate professional jargon and then seek to locate your "real" problem on a grid or map of respiratory, circulatory, or other-system problems.

Historians of ancient medicine classify the works of some ancient writers as comparable to these modern manuals since they list, describe, and discuss the "health" problems known to them in their own culture. Some writings of Hippocrates and Galen are often categorized in this way. Critics of this approach believe it to be medicocentric—that is, contemporary historians of medicine too often unwittingly impose modern scientific Western interpretations on these ancient texts.

Furthermore, some interpreters of biblical literature seek to use such ancient Latin or Greek resources in analyzing biblical texts. This strategy produces mixed results precisely because of the potential interpretative hazards just mentioned. Biblical authors themselves do not appear to have had at hand any of these ancient resources, nor do they use the same terminology as those authors. In fact, such ancient volumes may represent an elite understanding of human health misfortunes.

Biblical interpreters, therefore, fare better by taking seriously the reports of biblical authors and then resorting to both Mediterranean and medical anthropology for fresh insights to make sense of the admittedly meager data in biblical literature. Utilizing the tools of Mediterranean and medical anthropology, a biblical interpreter can construct a few different illness taxonomies from the data in Luke–Acts. The process involves designing an imposed etic view in the hopes of refining this until it becomes an etic perspective that is clearly derived from the etic data (Pilch 1996).

A TAXONOMY BASED ON SPIRIT INVOLVEMENT

The first taxonomy would embrace illnesses in which a spirit is involved. Modern Western readers of the Bible are struck by the frequent reports of spirit-possession and illness associated with spirits. Recall that Murdock (1980: 73) noted that belief in spirits is practically universal and shows no tendency to emerge in a particular ideational region, as do witchcraft theories. Recall also all the instances of spirit involvement in human affairs that appear in Luke's Gospel (see pp. 98–100). George Foster (1976) proposes a twofold taxonomy for illnesses in non-Western medical systems, based on whether or not spirits are involved. The insights of Murdock and Foster suggest that a spirit-focused taxonomy would fittingly address the New Testament data, but with a major modification for believers.

The New Testament associates some misfortunes with malevolent (unclean, evil, etc.) spirits. Since in this culture, every event must have a personal cause, if no human or malevolent spirit has caused it, one might presume that the other misfortunes should be ascribed to God. Thus Foster's taxonomy could be more appropriately modified to: illnesses in which a malevolent spirit is involved, and illness in which no malevolent spirit is involved (though God is or might be so perceived).

Several times in this book, we have noted that illness is understood in terms of misfortune. Such a concept is important here, because fortune or *mis*fortune in the world of Luke–Acts comes not from personal human activity but from the operation on humans by gods or spirits. This is a world in which the first question to be asked in the case of fortune or misfortune is *Who* did this to me? Hence, when we investigate a taxonomy of illness based on spirit involvement, we are tapping into a basic conception of the way the world works, namely, that a spirit (or god) has acted upon a mortal.

The Taxonomy Applied to Luke–Acts

As was observed above, Luke's worldview is heavily influenced by the perception of the activity of spirits, demons, and the like. In fact, this feature is more prominent in Luke–Acts than in the other Gospels. The activity of the spirits and demons is especially linked to sickness; Jesus heals those who are ill by means of the powerful, healing spirit of God.

To grasp the importance of this for our study of illness and healing in Luke, we turn to a passage found only in Luke. Jesus asserts: "Behold I cast out demons and perform cures today and tomorrow" (13:32). Casting out demons is not just another instance of healing but a way of describing the illness itself. By this association of the relationship of evil spirits and healing, Luke thus proclaims Jesus' identity as an exorcist. But *exorcist* is our term, an imposed etic concept; Luke considers Jesus' exorcisms as the healing of illnesses.

Let us not understate the amount or importance of spirit-related illness in Luke–Acts. Luke, of course, received many such stories from other Gospel traditions. For example, the other evangelists also report episodes of spirit-related illness:

Luke 4:33-37	(Mark 1:21-28)	man with the spirit of an unclean demon
Luke 8:26-39	(Mark 5:1-20)	man with a demon named Legion
Luke 9:37-43a	(Mark 9:14-29)	boy with a demon causing convulsions
Luke 9:49	(Mark 9:38-41)	another man casting out demons
Luke 11:14-15	(Matt. 9:32-34)	man with a demon making him mute
Luke 11:24-26	(Matt. 12:43-45)	Jesus' saying about unclean spirits

Table 6.1: Spirit-related illnesses common to Luke and another Evangelists

In addition to these, Luke adds his own reports of the presence and activity of spirits, demons, and Satan:

Luke 10:17	disciples against demons
Luke 22:3	Satan entered Judas
Luke 22:31-34	Satan wants to sift Simon
Acts 8:7	Philip casts out unclean spirits
Acts 12:23	Herod afflicted by an angel of the Lord
Acts 19:12	Paul's power exerted through handkerchiefs and cloths against evil spirits
Acts 19:14-16	seven sons of Sceva try to exorcise in Jesus' name

Table 6.2: Spirit-related illnesses unique to Luke

The malevolent presence of demons and unclean spirits in Luke–Acts is truly considerable.

In Luke's descriptions of ailments afflicting women, the spirit is given a very prominent place. As noted above, Peter's mother-in-law is afflicted by a spirit named Fever (4:38); among the women who follow Jesus, some were freed from evil spirits and infirmities (8:2-3); in the raising of Jairus' daughter, Luke notes: "Her spirit returned and she got up at once" (8:55); the stooped-over woman had a spirit of infirmity (13:10) and was bound by Satan for eighteen years (13:16). In Acts, Paul liberates a woman possessed by a spirit of divination (Acts 16:16). It should be obvious that in Luke's understanding and reports, spirit-possession looms very large, and healers such as Jesus, Peter, Philip, and Paul are able to address this human ailment with some measure of success.

A review of the summary statements in Luke–Acts detailing illnesses and summarizing healings does indeed reveal that possessions or spirit-caused maladies are one category of illness: Luke 4:40-41; 5:17; 6:18; 7:21, 22-23; 8:2-3; 9:1, 2, 10-11; 10:9, 17-20; 13:32; Acts 5:15-16; 8:6-7; 10:38; 19:11-12. It is important to keep in mind that even though spirit-related ailments form one category of illness, that is, one taxonomy, each episode must be interpreted on its own merit, for each will be distinctively different (Good and Good 1981).

A TAXONOMY BASED ON SYMBOLIC BODY ZONES AFFECTED

In our quest to learn how Luke and other inhabitants of his world perceived illnesses, we inquired about the parts of the body that tend to be afflicted with illness (see pp. 96–97). Again, let us not impose our scientific, Western viewpoint of how the body is perceived, but strive to learn how ancients understood and described the body.

Malina (1979; 1993: 63–89) formulated and developed a pattern of personality perception quite easily discernible among the largely Semitic biblical authors. Human beings are perceived as socially embedded and interacting personalities who react to persons and things outside them; in other words, they are not Western individualists. Biblical personalities, moreover, are not introspective and find it very difficult, if not impossible, to know what goes on inside themselves and others. "For the Lord sees not as human beings see; human beings look on the outward appearance, but the Lord looks on the heart" (2 Sam. 16:7).

This is a world where hypocrisy is considered a constant plague (see Pilch 1994), with the consequence that people are actually deceiving others by hiding their inner, evil thoughts behind a facade of orthopraxis (Luke 6:42; 12:1, 56; 13:15). They are like actors (the literal meaning of the Greek word *hypokritēs*) who refuse to be their authentic selves but rather play another role. Yet some powerful, prophetic figures, such as Jesus, penetrate this facade. Consider the significance of Jesus' comment in Luke 5:22, "Why do you question in your hearts?" He could read human hearts; he was not deceived by appearances (see also Acts 5:1-11). This has implications for Jesus' healings, for he can discern what illness is within, and he can read hearts to know what spirit is present. Healing, then, may require a physician who can discern spirits and inner states, as well as apply correct healing technique.

More to the point, however, people in the eastern Mediterranean world simply did not perceive human activity related to the same bodily organs that we do. Neither did they perceive the human body in the same way we do. In that culture, the individual person and the outside world with which that person interacts are described by using parts of the human body as metaphors. In fact, this body is divided into three zones of organs and behavior.

Zone 1	Emotion-fused thought. Westerners associate thought with the brain; not so the people in Luke's world. Human beings have hearts for thinking, together with eyes that collect data for the heart.
Zone 2	Self-expressive speech. Humans have mouths for communicating, along with ears that collect the communications of others. This activity is very important in biblical culture and receives a considerable amount of attention (see James 3:1-12).
Zone 3	Purposeful action. They have hands and feet for acting or behaving.

TABLE 6.3: Three symbolic body zones

	Bodily Parts	**Functions**
Zone 1	hearts–eyes	emotion-fused thought
Zone 2	mouth–ears	self-expressive speech
Zone 3	hands–feet	purposeful action

TABLE 6.4: Functions associated with body zones

According to Malina, these three zones describe human behavior throughout the Bible, from Genesis to Revelation. He presents a rather comprehensive list of the vocabulary that pertains to or reflects each zone. It will be of considerable importance to us as we read the narrative of illness and healing in Luke–Acts to attend to what bodily parts are ill. Correct understanding of the symbolic significance of eyes, ears, or hands may signal misfortune in regard to thought, speech, or action. (For an extensive list of this vocabulary, see Malina 1993: 74–75.)

This second taxonomy of illness based on symbolic body zones is able to cluster those reports in which specific parts of the body or their distinct activities are mentioned. Interpretation of the reports then hinges on noticing which zones are omitted, or which are healed, etc. Let us now apply this taxonomy to Luke's narrative.

The Taxonomy Applied to Luke–Acts

Our author reports thirty-one episodes of sick individuals involving twenty-three men and eight women, who are afflicted differently in terms of body zones. In the Gospel, men are afflicted in all three symbolic body zones. They are totally unhealthy, but Jesus is able to treat the full range of afflictions.

Heart–Eyes	7:21	Of Jesus it is reported that "on many that were blind he bestowed sight"
	18:35-43	A blind man near Jericho regains sight
Mouth–Ears	1:20, 64	Zechariah, father of John the Baptist, is stricken dumb, then regains his speech
	11:14-23	Jesus casts out a demon who was dumb
	22:47-54a	The ear of the high priest's slave is amputated, then healed
Hands–Feet	5:17-26	A paralytic is able to walk away healed in his feet and legs
	6:6-11	A man in a synagogue with withered right hand is restored to wholeness
	7:1-10, 11-16	The dead or near dead are restored to life; they who could do no activity whatever are given back that potential

TABLE 6.5: Illnesses of men in Luke according to symbolic body zones

The cases in Acts involving men reflect only two of the three symbolic zones (see Table 6.6).

Women in the Gospel reflect some distinctively feminine experiences, such as difficulty in conception (1:24, Elizabeth; 1:34, Mary) and menstrual irregularity (8:42b-48). This would pertain to the hand–feet zone, the zone of purposeful activity, since child-bearing and child-rearing are activities (a hands–feet function in this schema) committed to women in this culture. One woman, Jairus' daughter, is raised from the dead (8:40-42a, 49-56), which also pertains to the hands–feet zone. The dead can perform no purposeful activity; only the living can do that. Peter's mother-in-law is freed from a demon named Fever (4:38-39) and immediately begins to serve the

Heart–Eyes	9:18//22:13	Ananias heals Paul's temporary blindness
	13:1-12	Bar-Jesus, known also as Elymas, is made temporarily blind by Paul
Hands–Feet	3:1-10	Peter heals the man lame from birth at Beautiful Gate of the Temple
	9:32-35	Peter heals the paralytic Aeneas, bedridden for eight years
	14:8-18	Paul heals the life-long paralytic at Lystra
	28:1-6	Paul survives a lethal snake bite on the hand (see Luke 10:19)

TABLE 6.6: Illnesses of men in Acts according to symbolic body zones

disciples; this suggests that she, too, was affected in the hands–feet zone: lying in bed is to be deprived of foot and hand activity. The bent woman is freed from a spirit of infirmity (13:10-17) and is able to stand up straight again, suggesting yet another healing in the hands–feet zone. All of the women healed in Luke's Gospel, then, were healed in the symbolic body zone of hands–feet, the zone of purposeful activity. According to the Kluck-hohn-Strodtbeck model (see chapter 1), the primary value orientation for women in ancient Mediterranean culture is purposeful activity. Illness impeded these women from pursuing their dominant cultural orientation. Healing restores them to that capacity.

There are but two healings of women in Acts, and they give no significantly different picture. First, Tabitha is raised from the dead (9:36-43, the hands–feet zone), and a slave girl who was a soothsayer is purged of the evil spirit who prompts her to speak in this way (16:16-24, the mouth–ears zone). They are afflicted in the hands–feet zone as in the Gospel.

From this taxonomic description, we might draw some conclusions. The overall picture for men is that, whereas in the Gospel they are ailing in all three symbolic zones, in Acts the mouth–ears (consider all those speeches!) are problem-free, but heart–eyes (understanding) and hands–feet (actually doing, accomplishing) are still in the process of being healed. For women, specifically feminine ailments no longer plague them in Acts as they did in the Gospel. But the symbolic zone of purposeful activity (hands–feet) continues to require healing or empowering. Recall how in the Gospel Elizabeth and Mary composed canticles of praise and gratitude, and other women in search of healing were able to approach and dialogue with Jesus. The mouth–ears zone, which appeared healthy in the Gospel, needs healing in

Acts 16 because it has fallen under the domination of an evil spirit and is being exploited by men.

This latter observation suggests something known from studies on pain (see Pilch 1988a). Our biblical ancestors did not expect pain to be eliminated; it could only be alleviated. In a similar vein, healing was quite likely not expected to be lasting; very possibly the ailment could return later. Certainly this is obvious in the story of the spirit cast out who would return with seven more at a later time (Matt. 12:43-45). So it should not be surprising that Gospel women are quite wholesome in the mouth–ears zone, but at least one woman in Acts is presented as stricken in that very same zone and in need of healing. A reader needs to be constantly aware of the shifting context of each instance.

In the light of the reflections immediately preceding relative to the symbolic body zones, there were instances where a spirit-related illness was interpreted by means of the symbolic body zone taxonomy. This suggests that both taxonomies—the spirit-related taxonomy and the symbolic body zone taxonomy—could be collapsed into one. The unified taxonomy would have two sections that occasionally overlap. In this way, the dead could be considered as suffering from a hands–feet misfortune as well as a mouth-ears and heart–eyes misfortune, since nothing works in death!

Further, lepers or those afflicted with skin problems could also be considered as afflicted with a hands–feet illness since their malady excludes them from participating in the holy community, particularly at worship. Their purposeful activity, which is what the hands–feet symbolic body zone highlights, is severely limited. Indeed, the skin condition they called leprosy prevented them from performing the most purposeful activity known in their culture: joining the group in publicly acknowledging the One who has control over their existence.

In the final analysis, this holistic perspective on the illness category of human misfortunes in Luke–Acts prompts the observation that in the ministry of Jesus, all human beings (all three zones) are totally in need of God's redemption, which Jesus provides. When all zones are affected, this totality of zones correlates with the complete need for redemption. Persons totally dominated by Satan experience total powerlessness and, like people affected in all three zones, are also in need of redemption or empowerment. In Acts, since redemption is at hand in the preaching of the Gospel, zone two (mouth–ears) is trouble free, but the problems that remain are: correct thought/understanding (heart–eyes), since Peter identifies the killing of Jesus as ignorance, and Paul explains the Scriptures to people who do not understand (Acts 13); and what a believer should do (hands–feet)—walk like a follower of Jesus, be a follower of the Way. Even Acts 15 is a matter of doing. One important conclusion to be drawn from these efforts to heal the hands–feet symbolic body zone is to suggest that the Jesus movement is now a *halakah* that replaced earlier *halakah*.

A TAXONOMY BASED ON PURITY AND IMPURITY

Considering the difficulty that accompanies imagining skin problems (leprosy) as part of a taxonomy based on symbolic body zones, it is alternatively possible to construct a taxonomy of illnesses mentioned in the Gospels based on degrees of impurity (Malina 1981; Neyrey 1986b; Pilch 1981a). Skin problems called *leprosy* affect the body's boundary and thus symbolize threats to purity or wholeness. People with skin problems are considered impure (Lev. 13–14) because their body's boundary has been invaded and their presence in the community obviously violates the community's boundary. The presence in the community of people with skin problems makes it unclean, impure, and lacking in wholeness and holiness.

Men and women with uncontrolled or uncontrollable bodily fluids (Lev. 15) are also impure, as are people who come into contact with them. The woman with the uncontrollable flow of blood (Luke 8:42b-48), who touched Jesus' garment in hope of healing, was herself considered impure, and by touching Jesus rendered him impure as well. Jesus remedied her condition and restored her to purity, wholeness, and holiness, but he obviously did not consider himself adversely affected by her touch.

Similarly, people afflicted in one or another of the symbolic body zones can also be considered unwhole or impure because of their perceived lack of the symbolic bodily integrity that also points to a deficiency in purity, wholeness, holiness. The same could be said for those possessed, or affected in some way, by a malevolent spirit. Thus, a taxonomy based on impurity could be still another all-encompassing category for explaining the illnesses listed in the Gospels.

In each instance Jesus' therapeutic activity restores such afflicted individuals to purity, to wholeness. The practical outcome is that such healed individuals are also restored to full and active membership in the holy community, the people of God. This taxonomy can be developed in greater detail in another article.

To summarize, at least three different taxonomies can be constructed that would facilitate the understanding of health-misfortunes reported in the Gospels to guide the interpretation of healings narrated:

1. George Foster's taxonomy of illnesses based on the influence of a spirit or lack of such influence can be refined for interpreting biblical texts to

include illnesses associated with a malevolent spirit and illnesses presumably attributable to God's will, since God is ultimately responsible for everything that happens.

2. Another taxonomy can rightfully be based on the first-century, Mediterranean, tripartite understanding of symbolic body zones (hands-feet, heart-eyes, mouth-ears) that permeates the Bible from beginning to end. Many of the illnesses reported fit into such a taxonomy, and significant interpretations emerge—as noted above—by observing which zones remain unaffected and which zones seem amenable to therapeutic activity.

3. Finally, perhaps the most comprehensive taxonomy is one based on different kinds of impurity. This one could easily subsume the others taxonomies. Given the penchant of first-century Mediterranean people to judge one another on the basis of externals, a pure or whole person is one quite visibly clean, pure, whole. Anyone with a skin lesion (leprosy) is visibly unclean, not whole, impure. An individual possessed or affected by a malevolent spirit is similarly impure, unclean, not whole. Deficiencies in one or another of the three symbolic body zones are somewhat more difficult to judge; hence impurity based on the alleged malfunctioning of these zones could be a matter of dispute. A more detailed analysis would have to be pursued.

ILLNESS TAXONOMIES IN LUKE–ACTS AND THE CULTURAL VALUE PREFERENCE FOR BEING AND BEING-IN-BECOMING

Whatever taxonomy the investigator finally decides to construct, it will be important to remember that biblical people hold being as a primary value orientation (see chapter 1) and being-in-becoming as a close second choice. Being-in-becoming favors the development of all aspects of the self as an integrated whole. Integral harmony of the three symbolic body zones makes for a healthy and whole person. Ill people suffer a deficiency or malfunction in one or another of these zones. Ultimately, a sick person is restored to a proper state of being, not an ability to function.

But what of the hands–feet zone? Does it not bespeak activity, of doing? Certainly to some extent, but that is not the primary focus among first-century Mediterranean peasants. Healed paralytics in the Bible did not go job-hunting the very next day. Healing was viewed as restoration to integrity and wholeness, not necessarily to function. The healed paralytic was a whole person again. (On the importance of wholeness as a major value in Luke's world, see Neyrey 1986a: 142, 156–58.) Restoring the dead to life was the restoration to a preferable state of being, not a second chance at doing. A review of all the instances that are traditionally viewed as a restoration to doing can be better interpreted as the healing of the hands–feet zone and a restoration to a desirable state of being or being-in-becoming.

This important observation indicates that many of the healings or health concerns in the Bible concern a state rather than a function. In this, Luke and his Mediterranean world are quite different from modern, individualistic Westerners. Only if one knows the cultural clues will a considerate reader understand that the lengthy discussion of leprosy in Leviticus 13–14 concerns not activities or the ability to function but rather a state of being. At stake there is a description of who is unworthy to be part of the holy community, to approach the Lord in the holy place (Lev. 21:18). In this regard, the concerns are with states of being rather than functions. Persons who have a blemish, who are blind or lame, who have a mutilated face or a limb too long, an injured foot or hand, a hunchback , a sight defect, an itching disease or scabs, or crushed testicles, all of these are certainly capable of doing. But their specific condition describes a state of unwholeness and thus they are not permitted to join in the social behavior of group worship of God. Again, the issue is one of a state of unworthiness, not the loss of bodily activities. A Western observer whose culture favors doing over being would tend to interpret some of these handicaps as functional deficiencies. Even in today's world, such allegedly disabled individuals frequently reject this judgment because in many instances they are able to function. Biblical people prefer to view these same conditions as deficiencies in being or being-in-becoming.

BLINDNESS AND SEEING IN LUKE–ACTS

In light of the final observations, it should now be clear why restoration of sight seems to be an overarching motif in Luke–Acts. Healing activity in the New Testament is concerned chiefly with restoration to a wholesome and integral state of being; in Luke–Acts, while all three symbolic zones are healed, the chief focus seems to be on the heart–eyes zone.

At the beginning of the chapter we listed the instances of blindness in Luke–Acts. Within the scope of Luke and Acts, however, those occurrences are prefaced by Luke 4:18-19 and concluded by Acts 28:23-28. These two stories have to do with blindness and sight and they correlate with the formal notice of Jesus' mission and the rejection of that mission. These two stories are critically important to Luke's project, and they welcome examination from the modeling developed in this chapter. Luke 4:18-19 and Acts 28:23-28, then, are the premier cases of our inquiry. If our modeling is of any value, it must serve us well here.

We must pay attention to the beginning of Luke's Gospel and the end of Acts of the Apostles. Beginnings and endings are important rhetorical places, for in beginnings an author can condition a reader to perceive certain things, which are highlighted in the climax of the story, its ending. So it is with blindness and sight in Luke 4:18-19 and Acts 28:23-28.

At the beginning, only in Luke 4:18-19 do we find Jesus reading in the synagogue a prophetic text (Isa. 61:1-2) that is ordinarily considered to enumerate the kinds of healings that an anointed one of God would do and that indeed Jesus is reported as performing later in the Gospel (7:21-22). The passage is arranged in this fashion:

A bring good news to the poor
   B release to the captives/debtors
      C Sight to the blind
   B' release to the oppressed
A' announce a year of favor from the Lord

This concentric arrangement singles out blindness, a category of illness not involving malevolent spirit-aggression but affecting the heart–eyes symbolic body zone. This symbolic body zone and its function—sight, understanding, and related concepts—enjoys a central focus for Jesus' healing ministry in Luke–Acts.

The concluding verses of Acts (28:26-27) report Paul citing Isaiah once again, but this time Isa. 6:9-10, to describe the prominent individuals of the Jewish community who came to listen to his preaching but failed to be persuaded (see also Luke 8:9-15). The quote from Isaiah can be structured in this way:

Go to this people, and say:
   A You shall indeed hear but never understand
      B and you shall indeed see but never perceive
      B for this people's heart has grown dull
   A and their ears are heavy of hearing
      B and their eyes they have closed
      B lest they should perceive with their eyes
   A and hear with their ears
      B and understand with their heart
      B and turn to me to heal them

Of the three symbolic zones (A = mouth–ears, B = heart–eyes, C = hands–feet) of the human body, this passage fails to mention the hands-feet zone. The A lines refer to the symbolic body zone of mouth–ears, or self-expressive speech, while the B lines talk about the symbolic body zone of heart–eyes, or emotion-fused thought. This is significant because the illness or misfortune

at this point of Acts is precisely the failure of Paul's audience to hear and believe; the audience is sick in the area of emotion-fused thought. The phrase
turn to me refers to intellect or conscience and signifies conversion, a *heart*
rather than a *feet* activity. Clearly, in Luke–Acts, the worst misfortune consists in the failure to hear the word of God through prophets, angels, and
Christian preachers; failure to believe is sickness unto death. The Lukan
emphasis on illness in the zone of heart–eyes, then, would appear to be the
most serious illness, even an illness which defies healing.

By concentrating on blindness and seeing, we are touching the pivotal
issue of Luke: the correct understanding of Jesus as God's Christ, the change
of heart that is faith, and the correct insight into God's plan and purpose. In
a sense, Luke–Acts presumes that everyone is initially "blind" to Jesus, but
that Jesus can cure this illness, both by touch and by word.

While the hands–feet zone is amenable to healing in Acts—lame man (3:3-
10), bedridden paralytic (9:32-35), a born cripple (14:8-18), the boy who fell
out the window (20:7-12), innocuous snake bite on Paul's hand (28:1-6)—
the mouth–ears and heart–eyes zone do not yield so readily to healing. Even
though the blindness of some was remedied—Paul (9:18//22:13) and Elymas
(13:11)—others, such as Paul's Judaic visitors (28:25), chose to remain blind
by their refusal to understand the eloquent speeches of the preachers.

Together, the opening of Luke's Gospel and the closing of its companion
volume, Acts, form an inclusion for all the seeing/understanding (heart–eyes)
material contained in between. The correctness of this identification is confirmed by a statement that is found only in Luke in the context of Jesus' discussion with John's disciples: "In that hour he cured many of diseases and
plagues and evil spirits, and on many that were blind he bestowed sight" (7:21).

Some modern investigators would object to this conclusion. From a
modern, scientific medical perspective, their objection is that Luke's discussion of blindness vacillates between a physical condition (what really
happened) and a metaphorical or figurative application of that notion to
other human conditions such as ignorance and the like (what an interpreter chooses to include). This objection derives from a contemporary
medicocentric perspective that considers medical truth to be the only
truth. Such a perspective views human problems from a biomedical perspective and looks only for a disease, or a condition of physical blindness.
Recall that the ancient world did not possess this perspective. Reports of
human ailments in the biblical documents need to be interpreted within a
sociocultural framework (Good and Good 1981).

Luke, like all his contemporaries, describes not diseases but illnesses,
that is, sociocultural human conditions of anomaly, some of which have a

basis in a physical condition (like physical blindness) and others that would not have such a physical basis (like inability or refusal to understand/see arguments or evidence). The probable references to physical blindness or eye-conditions in Luke's Gospel are few and would likely include 4:18; 6:39; 7:21-22; 11:34-36; 18:35-43; as well as Acts 9:18//22:13; 13:11. But dispersed among these texts are many more references to sociocultural blindness or lack of understanding, and to seeing or understanding: parable about judging (6:39-42); parable of sower (8:9-16), parable of lamp (16-18); makarism on seeing (10:21-24); sign of Jonah (11:29-32), parable on lamp (33-36); signs in earth and sky (12:54-56) see Son of Man's day (17:22, 30); Herod hopes to see sign (23:8); crowds saw and beat their breasts (23:48); you are witnesses (24:48).

Acts takes up the Gospel's concluding note on seeing—"you are to be my witnesses" (1:8)—and continues this motif of sociocultural seeing indicating Luke's and his audience's stronger interest in sociocultural blindness than in physical blindness. Indeed, though they obviously knew the difference between physical and metaphorical blindness, the difference was not significant. Blindness of any kind was pitiful and to be remedied however possible. Thus Peter's citation of Joel 2:28-32 refers to the seeing of visions and dreams and then notes: "I (God) will show wonders in the heaven above and signs on the earth beneath" (Acts 2:19). The Greek words for wonders and signs *(terata kai semeia)* become a catch-phrase in Acts for validating the preaching of various individuals: Jesus (2:22); apostles (2:43; 5:12); Peter and John (4:30); Stephen (6:8); Moses in Stephen's sermon (7:36); and Paul and Barnabas (14:3; 15:12). All who saw were afraid; some believed, but others did not. Notice that in the Gospel, witnesses to Jesus and his activity seek (additional) signs (11:16, 29, 30; 21:7, 11, 25; 23:8), but in Acts, leaders and others recognize the import of the signs they have witnessed (4:16, 22; 8:6; 8:13), even if their response is sometimes less than appropriate.

It appears reasonable, then, to assert that blindness (both physical and sociocultural indiscriminately) is highlighted in the Luke–Acts taxonomy of illnesses as the chief problem to which Jesus and his followers brought relief.

CONCLUSION

Drawing upon models and concepts from Mediterranean and medical anthropology helps an interpreter to be a respectful reader of biblical material like Luke–Acts. The Mediterranean cultural preference for being or being-in-becoming recommends a definition of health that emphasizes a state of wholesomeness. The biblical culture's acceptance of spirits as operative and interfering in human affairs validates a division of human ailments into those involving malevolent spirits and those attributable to the spirit known as God.

Biblical culture's view of the healthy and wholesome human being as composed of three balanced symbolic body zones helps identify and categorize the ailments suffered that were presented for healing. Another look at the same material from the perspective of purity, wholeness, cleanness, and its opposites (impurity, uncleanness, and unwholeness) suggests perhaps the most comprehensive taxonomy of all: one based on purity concerns.

From the perspective of symbolic body zones, Luke appears to have singled out the heart–eyes zone as a leit motif in Luke–Acts, though the other dimensions also remain present. To my knowledge, these insights are unique contributions from the application of social-scientific models and concepts to the interpretation of biblical texts.

AFTERWORD

One avenue of research that might prove especially rewarding in the future would be the exploration of sickness reports in the Gospel from the perspective of a culture-bound syndrome: What precisely did Middle Eastern culture understand, for example, by paralysis? Inability to move the limbs is of course the physical problem. But what precisely were the consequences of this deficiency? How did this culture perceive and interpret the problem? We will have some opportunity to consider this in the next chapter on John's Gospel.

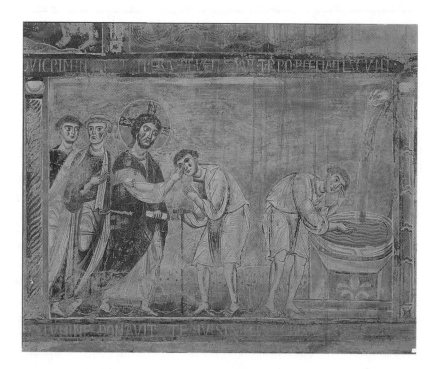

Jesus healing the blind man
School of Montecassino
San Angelo Formis, Capua, Italy

7

HEALING IN JOHN

As the previous chapters have indicated, much of Jesus' public reputation in the Synoptic Gospels derives from healing the sick. Terms for healing appear twenty-five times in Luke, seventeen times in Matthew, and eight times in Mark. By contrast, there are only three healing stories in the entire Gospel of John (4:46-54; 5:1-20; 9:1-41). Moreover, none of these healing stories actually underscores Jesus' reputation. Rather, healing in John reveals Jesus' true identity, and the focus of the interaction surrounding the healing report rests on controversy with opponents. This controversy is always revealing since it makes ever clearer who Jesus really is. The healing event itself fades into the background.

This relative scarcity of healing reports in John compared with the Synoptics requires us to modify our process of analysis. Using the definitions and insights presented earlier in the models for analyzing healing in the ancient world, we will analyze these three healing stories in some detail. To set them in proper Johannine context as presented in recent social-scientific investigations (Malina 1985; 1994; Malina and Rohrbaugh 1998), we begin by considering the character of John's community, for which he composed his Gospel.

THE EVANGELIST AND HIS COMMUNITY

John and his group are an anti-society. An anti-society is "a society that is set up within another society as a conscious alternative to it. It is a mode of resistance, resistance which may take the form either of passive symbiosis or of active hostility and even destruction" (Halliday 1978: 171; see also Halliday 1976). Therefore the language so patently peculiar to John's Gospel in contrast with the Synoptics is anti-language. The purpose of such distinctive in-group language is to bond members of John's community closer together and to assist them in understanding the way in which the glorified Jesus appears to them and functions in their life. While experiences of altered state of consciousness were quite common in the ancient Mediterranean world (Pilch 1998), it seems that they were especially frequent and significant in the Johannine community. Indeed, stimulating such experiences of the risen Jesus in alternate reality is a major expectation within the Johannine community.

The Jesus depicted by John is the one who has made the members of John's group children of God (John 1:12). They have become children of God by means of the life that Jesus imparts to those who believe in him (1:15). Hence when John describes Jesus' healings, it is essentially to depict how Jesus brought life to Israel and continues to do so in the Johannine group (10:10).

The story in John 4:46-54 points up Jesus' delaying reluctance to heal before returning to controversy with his Judean opponents, while in 5:1-20 and in the parallel story in chapter 9, the focus of the discussions falls directly upon Jesus in relation to work on the Sabbath. In other words, Jesus' healings in John's Gospel do not stir reactions to the healings themselves. The point rather is to highlight Jesus' true identity and to underscore the significance of the work entailed in the healings, whether that work is done by the person healed or by Jesus. Nonetheless these healings comprise three of the seven signs that are central to John's story.

The central concern in all sicknesses within traditional societies is the sick person's experience of being dislodged from his/her social moorings and social standing (see Lev. 13:46). This concern is especially salient in the healing interactions of John 5:1-20 and 9:1-41. In John 4:46-54 it remains in the background. Social interaction with family members, friends, neighbors, and village mates comes to a halt. To be healed is to be restored to one's social network. In the ancient Mediterranean world, one's state of being was more important than one's ability to act or function (see Pilch 1991c: 93–126). Thus the healers of that world focused on restoring a person to a valued state of being rather than to an ability to function. In other words, illness is not so much a biomedical matter as it is a social one. It is a matter of deviance from cultural norms and values and is therefore attributed to social, not physical causes. Healing in such a context is truly the restoration of meaning to life as medical anthropology has defined it.

Moreover, because sin is a breach of interpersonal relationships, it is clear why sin and sickness often go together. (Notice, however, that in 5:14 Jesus seems to accept that connection, while in 9:3 he rejects it.) Sin essentially consists of shaming or dishonoring another person (Pilch 1999: 59–64). For the sake of clarity it is useful to distinguish three hypothetical degrees. These degrees of dishonor depend upon whether or not the damage to the offended person's honor is revocable, whether or not the social boundaries can be readily repaired, and whether or not the implied or actual deprivation of honor is light, significant, or extreme and total. Thus transgressions of the boundaries that delineate a person in society run within these three degrees.

The first degree involves extreme and total dishonor of another with no possibility of revocation. This is outrage and would include murder, adultery, kidnapping, false witnessing, theft of vital goods or persons—total social degradation by depriving a person of all that is necessary for one's social status. These actions include all the things listed in the second half of the Ten Commandments, for this in fact is their content: outrages against one's fellow Israelites that are simply not revocable but require vengeance. The commandments forbid the taking of revenge.

The second degree involves a significant deprivation of honor. For example, one might not allow others to marry one's children even though one lets one's children marry theirs. Or, one might seek vengeance by stealing something not necessary to the livelihood of another. In such cases, revocation is possible, for example, by allowing the previously denied marriage, by restoring stolen items, by making monetary restitution for seducing someone's unbetrothed, unmarried daughter, and so forth.

The third and lowest degree of dishonor involves accidental withholding of the regular and ordinary interactions that require normal social responses. For instance: forgetting to repay a gift with one of equal or better value; inadvertently failing to greet a person of equal or higher status; and minor insults.

Thus, the experience of implicit or explicit dishonor must allow for satisfaction commensurate with the degree of dishonor present. Jesus, however, urges that dishonored people refuse to seek vengeance or satisfaction. He proposes forgiveness. In the Gospels the closest analogy for the forgiveness of sins is the forgiveness of debts (Luke 11:4; cf. Matt. 6:12), an analogy drawn from pervasive peasant experience. Debt threatened loss of land, livelihood, family. It was the result of being poor, that is, being unable to defend one's social position. Forgiveness thus has the character of restoration, a return to both self-sufficiency and one's place in the community. Since the introspective, guilt-oriented outlook of industrialized societies did not exist, forgiveness by God meant being divinely restored to one's position and therefore being freed from fear of loss at the hands of God. Conscience was not so much an interior voice of accusation as an external one—blame from the in-group, for example family, friends, neighbors or authorities (Luke 6:7; John 5:45; 8:10; see also 1 Cor. 4:4). Thus public accusation had the power to destroy, while forgiveness had the power to restore (Pilch 1999: 59–64).

In the context of health and well-being, the things that ailed people derived principally from socially rooted symptoms involving the person in society, rather than from organic and impersonal causes. Notice how in John's narratives, all symptoms are laid out as important, but the social ones receive special attention. The healing process is directly related to a person's solidarity with and loyalty to the overall belief system typical of the culture in general. The dictum in medical anthropology is: all healing is faith healing. If the client believes in and is loyal to the system, it can work, sometimes even to the amazement of scientists. Given the centrality of the Sabbath in Israelite ideology, one can readily appreciate the problem occasioned by Jesus' healing on a Sabbath, as evidenced in the controversies following such healing.

In John the connection between belief and healing is especially strong (4:50, 53; 8:24; 9:18, 35–36; 10:37-38; 11:42). Unlike the Synoptic Jesus, the Johannine Jesus heals on the basis of his interpersonal relationship with the Father. This relationship makes Jesus full of life, and he in turn volunteers to share that life with those to whom the Father sends him. Members of John's community, an anti-society, quite likely knew this from experience.

In order to be healed, a sick person is often urged to put his or her interpersonal relations in order. In John 5:14, Jesus seeks out the healed man to remind him that further breaches in interpersonal relations might cause even greater harm. Efficacy of the healing also requires community acceptance of a traditional healer's actions. In this story, however, when the healed man seeks such acceptance from the Judean community, the Sabbath controversy dominates the community's reaction (5:16).

THE HEALTHCARE SYSTEM

In John, as in the Synoptics, Jesus' activity is in the category of folk healing. Every society has provisions to deal with people who are sick. We call this the healthcare system (see Figure 2.1). Ancient physicians dealt with the symptoms a sick person manifested and sought to alleviate them and their consequences. There was no thought of eliminating anything (Pilch 1999: 72–78). In the first-century Mediterranean world these were physicians. Their approach to sickness was philosophical. This means that they studied the behavior of sick people and their symptoms and complaints, and developed theories to explain sickness. One thing they never did was touch, handle, cut, or otherwise physically minister to the sick. To this end they used slaves. Should the sick person die, the slave was killed—not the physician (see Horstmanshoff 1990).

Recall that in the popular sector, the concern and interest is to emphasize how illness affects and involves everyone in the kinship group and wider community. The consequences of healing, that is, restoring meaning to life, therefore affect this wider group as well, and all the more so in collectivistic society.

In the folk sector, the healer is a person who is recognized by people in a community as having the ability to restore people to health. This folk healer's "license to practice" is tacitly granted and acknowledged by each individual sick person and the local community. John's report that some doubted Jesus' abilities as a folk healer and questioned the source of his power (9:18) only highlights the limitations of a folk healer's abilities. As a folk healer, Jesus heals at a distance (4:50), heals by command (5:8), even touches his patients (9:6).

Recall that folk healers show these characteristics (see pp. 101–2 above):

1. The folk healer shares significant elements of the constituency's worldview and health concepts.

2. Folk healers accept everything that is presented (technically described as behavioral and somatic symptoms) as naturally co-occurring elements of a syndrome. The story of the man born blind (9:1-34) is a good example. That he sat begging where people passed by, that people thought his blindness was due to his own sin (9:34) or that of his parents (9:3), that his parents are constrained to admit his blindness from birth (and hence their probable sin)—these are all so many irrelevancies that a Western diagnostician (other than a psychiatrist) would put aside to focus on the real problem, the alleged damaged organ of sight. But the folk healer views everything as of equal importance. When John reports that the healed man was sought out by Jesus so that he might "believe in the Son of man," and not remain blind like the sighted Pharisees (9:40-41), we learn that for John's group part of therapy involved sharing in the attachment to Jesus along with the rest of the group.

3. The majority of folk healers treat their clients as outpatients. While in John, Jesus often does not have a crowd or audience for his healings, John's readers serve this role, thus bestowing honor on the Jesus to whom they are attached.

4. Folk healers take the patient's view of illness at face value. The pan-Mediterranean emphasis on visual dimensions of existence—this, after all, is central to honor, the core cultural value—may explain the prevalence of blindness and seeing, so emphasized in John 9 (blindness) and throughout the Gospel (seeing is believing).

5. The vocabulary folk healers use to describe an illness is invariably associated with the sick person's everyday experience and belief system.

6. Since folk healers are native to the community and know well its mores, history, and scandals, they make special use of the historical and social context of each illness. Jesus would know the official's son at Capernaum (4:46) since they lived in the same village, and in Jerusalem, the crippled man at the Sheep Gate (5:5) was a permanent fixture—perhaps for all thirty-eight years of his illness, while the blind man (9:1) made his living by begging.

HEALING IN JOHN: EXTREME CASES

Just as in the Synoptic Gospels, here in John as well, Jesus is described as a successful folk healer. Yet John's selection of Jesus' successes highlight truly extreme cases: a boy healed at a distance (4:46-54), a man crippled for thirty-eight years (5:1-20), a man born blind (9:1-41). The reason for this is that John is mainly concerned with having these events reveal who Jesus really is: one who heals because he is the source of life itself.

JOHN 4:46-54: A HEALING IN GALILEE: JESUS' SECOND SELF-DISCLOSURE

The first healing event of John's Gospel occurs in 4:46-54, which reports a healing in Galilee that in fact is Jesus' second self-disclosure, his second sign. In this Gospel, Jesus usually takes the initiative to help those whom he believes need his help, whereas in the Synoptics he normally does nothing unless he is asked to do so. In John, he is rarely approached by others for help. Yet in those few instances when people do in fact make requests, as here, Jesus' response is always one of delaying reluctance, followed by compliance and then a return to the conflict with the hostile Judeans. We find such a pattern in 2:1-11, 4:46-54, 7:2-14, and 11:1-16.

It is interesting to note that all of these requests come from in-group persons whose in-group status derives from birth or natural position: mother, town-mate, brothers, closest of friends. Yet it is only after a display of reluctance that Jesus eventually complies with their requests, and immediately afterwards engages Judeans in further conflict. In society (as opposed to anti-society) these in-group persons all deserve and receive immediate compliance. These in-group persons define the collective self and are really alter-egos of all members of the in-group. Perhaps John uses this pattern to inform members of his group about how to deal with their relatives and other natural in-group persons. The four examples of this pattern are shown in Table 7.1 (Giblin 1980).

2:1-14	4:46—5:1, 18	7:2-10	11:1-8
Request	*Request*	*Request*	*Request*
. . . When the wine failed, the mother of Jesus said to him, "They have no wine."	And at Capernaum there was an official whose son was ill . . . he went and begged him to come down and heal his son, for he was at the point of death.	So his brothers said to him, "Leave here and go to Judea, that your disciples may see the works you are doing.	Now a certain man was ill, Lazarus of Bethany. . . . So the sisters sent to him, saying, "Lord, he whom you love is ill."
Stalling Reluctance	*Stalling Reluctance*	*Stalling Reluctance*	*Stalling Reluctance*
And Jesus said to her, "O woman, what have you to do with me? My hour has not yet come."	Jesus therefore said to him, "Unless you see signs and wonders you will not believe."	Jesus said to them, "My time has not yet come, but your time is always here. . . . Go to the feast yourselves; I am not going up to this feast, for my time has not yet fully come."	But when Jesus heard it he said, "This illness is not unto death . . . So when he heard that he was ill, he stayed two days longer in the place where he was.
Compliance	*Compliance*	*Compliance*	*Compliance*
Jesus said to them, "Fill the jars with water." And they filled them up to the brim:	Jesus said to him, "Go; your son will live."	But after his brothers had gone up to the feast, then he also went up, not publicly but in private.	Then after this he said to the disciples, "Let us go into Judea again."
Conflict with the Judeans	*Conflict with the Judeans*	*Conflict with the Judeans*	*Conflict with the Judeans*
The Passover of the Judeans was at hand, and Jesus went up to Jerusalem. In the Temple he found people selling cattle, sheep and doves, and the money changers seated at their tables. Making a whip of cords he drove all of them out of the Temple.	After this there was a feast of the Judeans, and Jesus went up to Jerusalem. [healing at Bethzatha] . . . For this reason the Judeans were seeking all the more to kill him.	The Judeans were looking for him at the feast, and saying, "Where is he?" And there was considerable complaining about him among the crowds.	The disciples said to him, "Rabbi, the Judeans were but now seeking to stone you, and are you going there again?"

TABLE 7.1: C. H. Giblin's pattern

The healing story in 4:46-54 may be a variation on the healing story in Matt. 8:5-13 and Luke 7:1-10. It takes place in Cana, the location of the first sign that Jesus did in Galilee. Both signs elicit belief (2:11, 4:53). The Greek term *basilikos* is usually assumed to refer to a royal official, as it is often translated. The word, however, is simply the adjective royal. It could refer equally well to a royal personage, such as a member of the Herodian family. The latter seems more likely in view of the references to his whole household in 4:53 and to slaves in 4:51. In any case, whether a royal retainer or a royal aristocrat, the man whose son is near death would be very high on the Israelite social scale in a town like Capernaum. He is certainly not the type who would normally seek the patronage of a villager and artisan from Nazareth.

It is clear that the gossip network was at work spreading the reputation of Jesus. That someone of royal status would 'beg' (the term used when seeking a favor from a patron; note also the use of the polite term, 'Sir') for help from him is perhaps an indicator of Jesus' emerging status in the public mind. Since word of the aristocrat's begging would spread quickly in a small town, he risks serious public dishonor by doing so unless he is convinced of Jesus' abilities on the basis of his reputation. Such confidence in Jesus would certainly enhance the reputation of Jesus even more.

We do not know much about the boy's problem. He was ill (v. 46), at the point of death (v. 47). Evidence of his return to good health was when his fever left him (v. 52). It is futile to try to ascertain which of a range of sicknesses this might be. The fever here is not a demon as it very likely is in Luke's report of the problem afflicting Simon's mother-in-law (Luke 4:38-39). On the other hand, it is possible that the boy was suffering from the effects of the evil eye. Given the high mortality rate in the culture at this time, a healthy son would certainly be the object of envy, and thus an opportunity to exercise the evil eye (Elliott 1988; 1992; 1994).

In 3:16, 36 Jesus says that whoever believes will have new/renewed life. That, too, is the stated purpose of this Gospel (20:31). The triple repetition that the boy is alive (vv. 50, 51, and 53) indicates that this is precisely what has occurred in this episode. Jesus' healing activity gives the boy a new lease on life.

Jesus' Sabbath Healings

From the viewpoint of content, it might be useful to note how the author of John tells his stories of Jesus' Sabbath healings in chapters 5 and 9. As Neyrey (1995) has indicated, both passages have a rather large number of parallel features (see Table 7.2).

John 5	John 9
1. form: healing/controversy	1. form: healing/controversy
2. Jerusalem feast (5:1)	2. Jerusalem feast: Tabernacles
3. Sabbath healing (5:10)	3. Sabbath healing (9:14)
4. Old, proven infirmity (5:5)	4. Old, proven infirmity (9:1)
5. Illness and sin (5:14 "sin no more . . .")	5. Illness and sin (9:2 "who sinned . . .")
6. Site: a pool-Bethzatha (5:2)	6. Site: a pool-Siloam (9:7)
7. Command ("rise, take . . ." 5:7) obedience/healing (5:9)	7. Command ("go, wash" 9:7a) obedience/healing (9:7b)
8. Court of inquiry (5:9b-16) healed man court of inquiry charge: Sabbath violation defense (5:31-47)	8. Court of inquiry (9:13-34) healed man court of inquiry charge: Sabbath violation defense (9:30-34)
9. Ideological issue: belief Question: who is he? (5:12-13) he did not know	9. Ideological issue: belief Question: where is he? I do not know (9:12) Question: What do you say about him? a Prophet! (9:17)
10. Subsequent meeting Jesus found him (5:14) no Christophany report to Judeans about Jesus (5:14)	10. Subsequent meeting Jesus found him (9:35) Christophany (9:35-38) Do you believe? Lord, I believe (9:35-38)
11. Judgment: tables turned they judge Jesus (5:9-16) Jesus judges them (5:38-47)	11. Judgment: tables turned they judge Jesus (9:13-34) Jesus judges them (9:39-41)

TABLE 7.2: Parallel features in John 5 and 9

John 5:1-20: The Sabbath Healing of a Paralytic

The story in 5:1-20 is the first appearance of a theme that will become a major motif in the remainder of John's Gospel: conflict between Jesus and the Judean leadership. The story opens the section about how Jesus' bringing life to Israel provoked controversy. Here (vv. 1, 10, 15), as elsewhere in John, it is important to correct the anachronistic translation 'Jews' (see Pilch 1999: 98–104). 'Judeans' was the customary term used by outsiders to describe members of the house of Israel, wherever they might live.

It is not clear which particular festival brings Jesus to Jerusalem this time. Earlier, he had been there for Passover (2:23). The Sabbath healing in this story will remain a matter of controversy (7:23) when he returns to Jerusalem again for the Feast of Sukkoth/Tabernacles (7:2).

The story opens with the sick man by the pool. Sick persons were here not only to seek healing but also to beg. Such beggars were among the socially expendable, the unclean "throw-away" peoples that could be found in every pre-industrial city. Included in this same category were prostitutes, the poorest day laborers, tanners (forced to live outside the cities because they reeked of the urine used in the tanning process), peddlers, bandits, sailors, hustlers (for example, gamblers, usurers), ass drivers, dung collectors, and even some merchants. It was customary to force such persons out of the cities at night when gates were locked. They returned during the daytime to beg or find work. These people without social standing (we would see them as the "poorest") lived just outside the city walls or along the hedgerows of adjacent fields. While they constituted perhaps not more than 10% of the total population, their living conditions and life chances were simply appalling by modern standards. Verse 4, which provided an explanation for the healing power that came with the stirring of the waters (v. 7), is almost certainly not part of the original text; translations invariably put it in a footnote.

The sick person in this story is completely incapable of maintaining even a minimally honorable social position. From a Mediterranean point of view, he was poor, since by definition being poor in this culture means being unable to maintain one's social standing. The sketchy details of John's report do not tell us how the man, who had been sick for thirty-eight years, survived. There is no implication in verse 6 or elsewhere that he had been at the pool for the entire thirty-eight years. He apparently was able to get around, although very slowly since he could never beat anyone else to the water (v. 7). There is no explanation of how he was fed or how he came to the pool on a daily basis from wherever he was living.

The man's acknowledgment that he had "no one" to put him in the pool is mind-boggling. If this is not hyperbole, it is difficult to imagine someone without family, given the large, extended families that are common in the Middle East. If it is a direct and truthful admission, he indeed does not have next of kin (redeemer) who would be obliged to help him (see Num. 25:25). On the other hand, if he has been at this pool a long time, it is similarly mind-boggling that he has not made a friend who might help him. Making friends is a major occupation for the Mediterranean male. It is indeed difficult to imagine how a beggar in such a position could survive at all! He is desperately in need of healing, of restored meaning for his life.

John does not explain how he knew that the man had been at the pool for a long time. It would, of course, be a topic of the loud conversations of others at the pool. The sick man's reply to Jesus makes painfully clear his friendless and therefore hopeless situation. It could also imply that he is wondering whether Jesus might become the needed friend to put him into the pool. Since the sick man does not know who is talking to him, he obviously does not anticipate being healed by Jesus. Instead, his focus remains on the therapeutic powers of the stirred water.

Jesus' command to the healed man to walk away with his mat is a clear direction to break one of Israel's Sabbath regulations mediated by Moses and emphasized by Jeremiah: "Thus says the LORD, take heed for the sake of your lives, and do not bear any burden on the Sabbath day or bring it in by the gates of Jerusalem. And do not carry a burden out of your homes on the Sabbath or do any work, but keep the Sabbath day holy as I commanded your fathers" (Jer. 17:21-22). The literalist reading of the Torah notices that God's final action after creation was to rest: "So God blessed the seventh day and hallowed it, because on it God rested from all the work that he had done in creation" (Gen. 2:3). In this understanding, the present age of creation is precisely this seventh day. For scribal Pharisees, God is resting at present, just as Moses had said. Jesus' claim that God is working even now (5:1) is the point that stirs his opponents anger against him.

Jeremiah's explanation of the Sabbath command sets forth the prohibition of "servile work"—work done by slaves in elite households. The Sabbath was viewed as a weekly replication of the annual Passover that celebrated Israel's status as free persons. In the present age, these freed Israelites are devoted to the service of their liberator God. On the Sabbath Israelites were to behave like free elites—even if their actual status was not elite—free for the service of their God alone. The healed man, very plausibly an Israelite, carries his mat around so publicly that his actions come to the attention of the Judeans. In their eyes, it is clear that he is breaking God's law. This controversy between Jesus and the Judeans over law-breaking (and later, over Jesus' claims of kinship with God) will eventually lead to Jesus' death.

Observe that in 9:2 Jesus rejects the idea that suffering is payment for sin, while here in 5:14 he seems to accept it. If one assumes that Jesus' reference to something worse happening to the man is a reference to his illness, Jesus seems to be threatening another disease if the man should sin again. But if we recall that in Mediterranean societies sin is a breach of interpersonal relations, the apparent contradiction between John 5 and 9 disappears. If sin is anything that destroys one's relationship with the group, and if we remember that this man had no friends to put him into the pool, Jesus' comment makes perfect sense. As a friendless outcast, the man was indeed a sinner, an outsider unattached to a group. He may have been sick, but he was also ill. This means that he may well indeed have had a genuine, physical problem, perhaps even a handicap. But bereft of group-attachment of any kind (neither family nor friends, as the text implies), his life in collectivistic society has lost its meaning. Illness is the loss of meaning in one's life. Healing restores meaning, all the time, infallibly. Given his age and the short life expectancies in antiquity, should the man repeat whatever disrupted his relationship with the group, he would indeed risk the worst of all fates: having no one to bury and remember him.

Some commentators suggest that the healed man is actually ungrateful since he runs to tell the Judeans of Jesus' identity as soon as he learns it. That may be so, but having been accused of law-breaking himself, it is more plausible that the healed man seeks that crucial item he has not had for the last thirty-eight years: attachment to the dominant social group. These are, of course, the enemies of Jesus. The man's breach with them could only be re-established if he acts quickly and decisively.

With regard to the conflict over Sabbath activity, Jesus says it exists only because his Judean opponents are unaware of the fact that God continues to work, even on the Sabbath. How can human beings confine God's activity to six days? In John's Gospel, only Jesus uses works (Greek: *erga*) to describe his activities. The significance of this is that in the Septuagint, *erga* describes the actions of God, chief of which are creation and redemption. Translated into a different register, creation is the act of giving life, and redemption is the restoration of meaning to life (Neyrey 1988: 74–76). The seven signs or works that Jesus performs in John illustrate each of these. Jesus gives life to the official's son (John 4) and to Lazarus (John 11), while feeding (John 6) is also an action of sustaining life. Jesus enhances the meaning of life at the wedding in Cana (John 2), for the paralytic (John 5), when he walks on the sea demonstrating mastery over nature (John 6), and when he restores sight to the man born blind (John 9). In John, Jesus as healer restores to life and restores meaning to life.

In the concluding verses, mention of God's activity (works) is associated with the topic of life in face of death and with Jesus' claims to kinship with God. The cluster of these topics fuel the ongoing controversy between Jesus and the Judeans until his death. Keep in mind that honor derives from one's family. Kinship claims are therefore always honor claims (genealogies are a good example; Hanson and Oakman 1998: 26–31). When Jesus claims kinship with God, he is claiming God's honor for himself. The reaction of his Judean opponents is therefore not surprising; they would have been truly astounded by such a claim. Of course, members of John's anti-society were not.

These verses, therefore, represent an important kinship statement in which the ancient dictum is reaffirmed: like father like son. Kinship is not only a matter of biology, but also a matter of loyalty and solidarity. As Jesus says in 10:30, "The Father and I are one" (also 14:10). The language about doing what he sees the Father doing evokes the picture of a workshop apprentice in which the son learns directly from his father. The first of the works of the Father which the Son now does (v. 21) is the giving of life.

The statement in v. 20 that the Father loves the son (see also 3:35) conjures up images of family affection for Western readers. We imagine it to be a description of an inner, psychological state. Entire Christologies have been constructed around notions such as these. Using modern psychology and our psychological orientations to interpret the Bible, however, is inappropriate (Pilch 1997). In the group-oriented Mediterranean society, the term love describes attachment or loyalty (especially group attachment) and the behavior that goes along with it. The emotion of affection may or may not be included, but it is not the primary meaning of the word. To "love your neighbor as yourself" (Matt. 19:19) means that one should be attached to the people in one's neighborhood or even one's ethnic group as to one's own family (see Lev. 19:17-18). The Greek tense that Matthew uses implies continuous action, that is, ongoing loyalty.

John 9:1-41: The Sabbath Healing of a Man Born Blind

The next healing in John is described in 9:1-41. This story of how Jesus' healing of a man born blind instigates controversy is the opening event in that section of John's Gospel telling of how Judeans reacted to Jesus' bringing light and life to Jerusalem (9:1—10:42). The author situates this incident directly after Jesus leaves the temple area with his disciples. Presumably Jesus is present in Jerusalem because of the feast of Sukkoth/Tabernacles, which provides the occasion for his self-presentation to Judeans as the light of Israel. By restoring sight to the blind man, Jesus further highlights his role as bringer of light/life.

While the blind man receives both the ability to see physically and to understand—that is, he gains intellectual insight—Jesus' opponents ultimately will be overcome with darkness. They will become blind. The two will have exchanged positions.

The author's description of this story begins with an introduction (vv. 1-5), followed by four episodes through which the event unfolds: first the healing (vv. 6-12), then a first interrogation of the newly sighted person (vv. 13-17), followed by the interrogation of his parents (vv. 18-23) and a second interrogation of the healed man (vv. 24-34), and bracketed by a conclusion (vv. 35-42) matching the introduction.

The model that best serves to assist in analyzing this story is that of symbolic healing (see pp. 32–34 above). Western readers whose thinking is dominated by modern scientific medicine tend to focus on the physical condition, blindness, and seek to investigate what kind of blindness could have been ameliorated in this encounter. People interpret reality within their particular cultural contexts. Such socially shared interpretations, largely metaphorical, are usually identified with the realities they interpret. In this sense they are quite real in their effects. Hence medical anthropologists agree that the metaphorical structure of a culture is as decisively effective as physiological or pharmacological elements. What Jesus the healer does is mediate culture. Let us consider John 9 as it reflects the four essential structural stages involved in symbolic healing.

Stage 1. Building a Symbolic Bridge. A symbolic bridge links personal experience (for example, blindness), social relations (intra-family, with neighbors, and with the Pharisees), and cultural meanings (sin, light, life). The blind man's experiential reality (like that of his culture) is an interpreted, hence mythic, world. It may or may not be empirically true, but it certainly is experientially true. The dialogue of the story establishes this bridge.

The notion that sin caused suffering was widely accepted in the New Testament period (cf. Luke 13:2; consider the debate over this idea in the book of Job [e.g., 22:5-11; 34:5-9], centuries earlier). Stereotypical thinking at the time explains how Israelites concluded that given the justice of God, suffering could only be the result of some sin, whether conscious or unconscious. The later rabbinic tradition expressed it thus: "There is no death without sin and no suffering without iniquity" (*b. Shabbath* 55a). Punishment inflicted from birth, however, was a different question. A different explanation would be needed. Surely, the individual could not have sinned. On the other hand, collectivistic sin could not be ruled out. Moreover, since individuals in this culture were collectivistic individuals, collectivistic sin made good sense.

Two explanations were possible. On the basis of Exod. 20:5, some Israelite scribal teachers argued that the sins of the fathers were responsible for the suffering of their children. Hence a child could be born blind because of the misconduct of its parents. Much later in the rabbinic tradition, other teachers argued that it was precisely prenatal sin on the part of the child that brought on such calamities (*Genesis Rabbah* 63.6)! How is this possible? If a pregnant woman worshiped an idol, for example, the fetus was said to do the same (*Song of Songs Rabbah* 1.41). In v. 34, then, the opponents assert this connection between sin and blindness, but in 9:3 Jesus rejects such explanations (compare John 5:14).

Light is another key symbol in this mythic world, and especially in the mythic world of John's community. In antiquity, light was stuff. It was its own source. As the creation story indicates, light did not need the sun in order to exist. The light in a human being was considered living light as opposed to the light of the sky. This living light derived from the heart and emerged from the eyes in the seeing process. The eyes were made of fire, the stuff that causes light. When this fire emanated from the eyes, the human person was able to see. Jesus observed: "The eye is the lamp of the body" (Matt. 6:22). Aristotle said: "Vision is fire" (*Problems* 31, 959b); "Sight (is made) from fire and hearing from air" (*Problems* 960a). To be blind was to have eyes from which darkness emanated. Darkness was the presence of dark (also stuff) rather than the absence of light. Blind people were people whose heart was full of darkness, hence from whose eyes dark emanated. Blind people were invariably suspected of possessing and giving the evil eye (Matt. 6:22-23).

Light is also associated with life. The Hebrew of Job 33:30 speaks of the "light which gives life" (also Ps. 56:13). When Jesus says he is the light of the world, he is saying that he both enables Israel to see the ways things really are, and that he is the source of Israel's life. In John, *world* refers to Israel (see 18:20). Jesus is the authentic vision of existence. He comes to bring life. Just as God has life (5:26) so does the Son have life in himself (5:26). Jesus is the bread of life (6:48), the living resurrection (11:25), and even his words are life (6:63). His purpose for coming was that his followers "might have life, and have it abundantly" (10:10)

The word *life* appears forty-seven times in John (while only six times in Matthew, three times in Mark, five times in Luke). Jesus' works or signs are all about life. He changes inert water into wine, a living liquid (consider its effects!). Nicodemus, once born, is invited to be born from above, which would mean being born anew. The Samaritan woman appreciates the difference between water in a well and the living water Jesus gives (readily understandable as rain that falls from the realm of God and the angels). The young son of an official is told he will live. Jesus associates bread, bread from the sky (manna), and living bread, that is, life-giving bread. A blind man (equivalent to being dead) regains his sight, which is animated light, a synonym for life! Above all, Jesus dies to give life.

Stage 2. Relating the Sick Person to the Mythic World. Jesus accomplishes this in the dialogue. To his disciples he explains that he will work the works of the one who sent him; those are life-giving and meaning-restoring works (see above, pp. 127–31, the discussion of *works* in John 5). Jesus also declares that he is the light of the world. After anointing the man's eyes with mud, Jesus sends him to the pool of Siloam. At the end of the story when Jesus finds the man again, the man confesses his loyalty to Jesus ("Lord, I believe"), which is faith/loyalty in the mythic world. That Jesus has activated the symbolic connections between the man's blindness and his mythic world is evident in the dialogs that intervene between Jesus' two encounters with the man. The parents, neighbors, Pharisees, and hostile Judeans are all aware of the connections Jesus has made. Of course, some accept the connections while others don't.

Stage 3. Transactional (or Mediating) Symbol. The author now describes Jesus' healing action in which he uses spittle and mud as transactional symbols. The symbol is particularized from the general meaning system and guides the therapeutic change in the blind man's emotional reactions. Jesus generalizes the blindness (personal experience equivalent to death) into the therapeutic meaning system (animated light, a living entity), and the blind man particularizes the symbolic meaning (Jesus, the light of the world, gives sight/life and insight to the blind man). The transaction works because participants in symbolic healing share mutual expectations that shape and name the illness, in this case blindness.

Jesus' behavior here is typical of ancient folk healers. He uses saliva (see also Mark 7:33; 8:23) because it was widely believed that saliva gave protection particularly against the evil eye, which perhaps the majority of people there would have assumed the blind man possessed. Even in the contemporary Mediterranean world, saliva is often used to protect children from the evil eye (Elliott 1994). A common parental response to a compliment given carelessly to her/his child is to bite the knuckle of the index finger, then spit three times.

It was a widespread belief in antiquity that sharing saliva was a form of blood covenant that could be protective. Pliny notes that spittle from various sources, including human spittle, has special curative powers (*Natural History* 27.75; 28.5, 48, 61, 77; 29.12, 32; 32.29). Tacitus states that a blind man once sought a cure by applying the spittle of the emperor Vespasian to his eyes (*History* 4.8).

Even though modern commentators observe that the explanation of the term *Siloam* as meaning 'sent' lacks a clear etymological basis, the explanation serves John's anti-societal purposes well. Jesus is said to be sent from the Father more than fifty times in John's Gospel. This is the language of patronage: the patron sends the broker on errands. If God has sent Jesus, then Jesus is God's broker. The blind man will soon mediate this information to the authorities.

The first people to be surprised in this story are the healed man's neighbors and those who had seen him begging. Beggars were present in every ancient city. They were considered expendable. Forced to live outside the city, most of them came into the streets during the daytime in order to beg. The fact that people could not agree on the actual identity of the healed man indicates that he was very loosely connected to the community at large. (The sick man in 5:1-18 was in a similar position.) The healed blind man's acknowledgment that he does not know Jesus' whereabouts indicates that he is not yet part of Jesus' following. He only knows Jesus' name, which he plausibly heard while he was begging.

The Pharisees are the first to formally interrogate the newly sighted man. They are caught between two important concerns (9:13-17). The first is Jesus' disregard of the Sabbath prohibition of work (alluded to vv. 3-4, with the note that it is the work of God; cf. 5:17 and discussion of works above). Babylonian rabbis of an era long after Jesus' time would argue that one should not anoint an eye on the Sabbath (*b. Abodah Zarah* 28b). The opinion of Israel's sages reported in the Jerusalem Talmud (*j. Shabbath* 14d; 17f) is that a person not put fasting spittle on anyone's eyes on the Sabbath day, perhaps because no one is to fast on the Sabbath. The healed man articulates another concern that disturbs them: How can a man who is a sinner perform such signs? According to the prevalent ideology of reward and punishment (see vv. 1-2), a sinner should be suffering, not performing signs.

The vigorous difference of opinion now leads the newly sighted man to a new stage of enlightenment. He realizes that Jesus is a prophet and identifies him as such. It is possible that in John's group, this is a first stage in recognizing Jesus. It also occurs in 4:19; 6:14; 7:40. From this recognition of Jesus as prophet in Israel, the healed man next recognizes him as the Son of Man (9:35), the "Sky Man" who provides access to the realm of God in the sky (1:51). Quite extraordinary is the fact that the Pharisees (persons of the retainer class) are asking the blind man (someone from the degraded class) a question of any significance at all. This just doesn't happen. The Greek pronoun in their question (What do *you* say) is emphatic. Clearly, they recognize that the healed man is beginning to play the broker role for which *he* was sent.

Next the parents are interrogated (9:18-23). Their statements about their son's blindness strengthen the connection of his illness to the mythic world Jesus calls upon to heal this condition. One senses that the parents have accepted that connection, for they fear acknowledging Jesus as effective (as Messiah), considering the consequences. The fear of expulsion, of course, is an anachronism from late in the first century, reflecting the debate at that time between the disciples of Jesus and the disciples of Moses (see vv. 28-29). It may also reflect the twelfth of the so-called Eighteen Benedictions, which apparently excluded Israelite followers of Jesus from synagogue gatherings. John's story draws such boundaries and sharply marks off his anti-society from Judean society, which is an overarching concern in his Gospel.

The newly sighted person now faces a second round of interrogation from the Pharisees (vv. 24-34). A basic obligation of a client was to praise his patron in public. By asking the healed man to honor God, then adding that Jesus is a sinner, the Pharisees are urging him to recognize God as patron but reject Jesus as an authorized broker. This interrogation further confirms the efficacy of Jesus' healing intervention.

The healed man shows himself to be quite a savvy and capable man of his culture. The form of his question to the Pharisees in Greek ("Do you also want to become his disciples?") implies that he expects a negative answer. All questions in the Middle East are a challenge to honor, but this is an especially sharp public honor challenge. An effective response to such a challenge, especially from someone in a lower social status, is to pour sarcasm on the challenger. The implication is that he is so low in status, he does not warrant a direct response. Recall that Jesus treated the Canaanite women's petition with dead silence. He ignored her because she was in no way his equal and thus ineligible to play the game of challenge and riposte (Matt. 15:23). The Greek term used here in John 9:28 *(loidoreo)* means to speak publicly in a highly insulting manner.

The healed man's rejoinder about where Jesus is from is yet another skillful link of his new situation to its likely source, namely, from God. Not only does it add yet another testimony to the efficacy of what Jesus did for him, but it also strengthens the link of the blind man's ameliorated condition to the mythic world that he and Jesus recognized and agreed upon, namely, the world where one can contact God's works of giving life and restoring meaning to life.

The healed man forces recognition of one side of the dilemma posed in v. 16. A sinner could not broker God's beneficence. The healed man clearly wins the honor challenge. That his shamed opponents seek to throw him out is an admission they have lost the game. Their wits have failed. This is extremely shameful in a culture where one proves manliness not only by physical prowess but especially by mastery of language and beating other men in word games (recall Samson in Judges 14).

The healed man's insight continues to grow to the same degree, it would seem, that the obstinacy of Jesus' opponents also grows. The healed man now knows Jesus is from God and is obedient to him. Meanwhile, the blindness of the opponents continues to worsen. They have no idea where Jesus is from, which means they do not even have the most basic information about him. That is what knowing where a person is from provides in this culture.

Stage 4. Confirmation. Jesus confirms the transformation of the particularized symbolic meaning. The healing (the equivalent of meaning–restoring) interaction fosters this transformation as a work of culture. Jesus has transformed the psychophysiological process (whatever it may have been in this instance) into meaningful experience (regained sight and fresh insight, entitlement to be fully restored to the community, ability to enter into full fellowship with Jesus and his followers).

Success is affirmed in vv. 35-41, which form a conclusion that brackets the introduction in reverse order (a chiasmus). Jesus' question to the healed man asks if he believes 'into' the Son of Man. The idea of believing 'into' Jesus, in John's anti-language, implies loyalty to a very high degree. In actuality, Jesus is asking whether the man is prepared to become a member of his anti-society. He becomes a full-fledged member in v. 38.

By calling Jesus "Sir" (v. 36), the healed man recognizes and accepts Jesus as his patron. The decision is repeated in still more graphic terms in v. 38, when he not only repeats this customary title for patron, but also offers a traditional patronage gesture. The Greek term *(proskyneo),* translated "worship" by the NRSV, is widely used in the ancient world to describe the gesture of falling down before a person and the kissing the hem of his garment, or his feet, or the ground on which he walked. This was the appropriate way for clients to ask favors of a patron.

The concluding comments of Jesus complete the notion of reversal. The blind see and the seeing have become blind (cf. Isa. 6:10; 42:19-20; John 12:40). The ill are healed; the healthy become ill. The Greek form of the Pharisees' question ("Are we also blind?") implies the expectation of a negative answer. Jesus gives them credit for still retaining sufficient sight/insight to recognize that they are accountable.

The final word in this passage, *remain* (sometimes also translated 'abide'), is a key term in John. Most of the time it describes solidarity with Jesus and his faction. Its contrary use here draws a sharp distinction between the Pharisees and the followers of Jesus.

CONCLUSION

To read these accounts as stories of healing in John, to list them among the works of Jesus the healer, and to explain them in terms of healing models befitting the first-century Mediterranean world, all this would be highly informative. But for John's anti-society, such an assessment of Jesus' healing at a distance, of Jesus' restoring mobility to a man severely lame for thirty-eight years and restoring sight to a man born blind is quite beside the real point. In John's group, Jesus is the source of life and light, of the wholeness created by God at the beginning and maintained by God in the present, God's ongoing Sabbath. For persons in John's group whose relatives are ill or who themselves suffer from forms of immobility and blindness, the experience of the living Jesus in midst of the group brings restoration. It is access to the resurrected Messiah of Israel in altered state of consciousness (ASC) experiences that enables results such as those reported in the significant healing interactions of Jesus (Pilch 1998).

AFTERWORD

In view of my increased awareness of the significance of life that the risen Jesus makes available in John's anti-society, it would now seem a worthwhile effort to investigate the raising of Lazarus from the dead, along with other such reports in the synoptic Gospels.

Jesus healing the sick
Rembrandt Harmensz van Rijn
The Hundred Guilder Print, 1649

CONCLUSION

IN 1994, A PHYSICAL EXAMINATION DISCLOSED that my wife had an advanced stage of ovarian cancer. She underwent surgery within a week, and the surgeon was confident he had removed 95 to 97 percent of the disease. Nevertheless, the regimen required a follow-up of six chemotherapy treatments. During these treatments, tests indicated the therapy was effective. At the end of the treatments, the oncologist said:

"According to the tests, you are definitely in remission."

"Oh," she asked, "do you mean that I am cured?"

"No," he responded. "We can't use that word until you are in remission for five years."

She was in remission for about one year. Then the cancer recurred, and even though treatments continued, she died approximately three years after the disease was initially discovered. This is the average life expectancy of a person with ovarian cancer that is discovered at an advanced stage.

As modern Western medicine admits, cure is a relatively rare occurrence in human experience. For most of the twentieth century, human sickness has peaked and subsided before modern science discovered a cure. Often the human body accommodates and learns how to defeat the sickness. In some cases this takes longer than in others.

Healing, on the other hand, occurs always, infallibly, 100 percent of the time. Healing is the restoration of meaning to life. All people, no matter how serious their condition, eventually come to some resolution. My wife was healed even before she went into remission and continued in her healed state until she died. She and I together discovered new meaning in life, meaning specific to this shared experienced of battling the disease, and ultimately—in our case—recognizing that the disease had won.

Medical anthropology coined and refined these concepts of curing and healing. They are widely known and understood, particularly among people trained for pastoral care with the sick. How surprising then, at a conference of professionals involved in healthcare delivery, that when the speaker reviewed these terms and asked: "From this perspective, did Jesus ever cure anybody?" there was a pause and a gasp. "No" would be a historically and scientifically correct answer. "We have no way of knowing" would also be an acceptable answer, preferable for many. Yet some who attended this conference insisted: "Yes, absolutely, without a doubt." The surprise here is that those who otherwise would not dare make such a judgment without laboratory tests before and after modern treatment seemed to experience no difficulty making a positive assertion about antiquity without such evidence. In the New Testament we have no certain knowledge about the exact nature of most of the health problems people presented to Jesus.

The discussion of leprosy in chapter 3 should assure anyone who still has doubts about the value of the terms: *cure, heal, disease, illness* as defined by medical anthropology. Since no physical evidence for true leprosy (disease) in ancient Palestine has yet been found, it seems reasonable to conclude that Jesus very likely did not cure anyone of this disease. He did heal those afflicted with this problem by reintegrating them into society. He restored meaning to the lives of these collectivistic persons. Thus the terms and definitions given to us by medical anthropology seem eminently useful for reading narratives about sick people and their illnesses in the Bible with appropriate respect for their culture and their lives long before scientific medicine developed. The modern Western reader has little awareness of the degree of sophisticated medical knowledge she or he possesses from the newspapers, television, and other sources. Add this to the Western, particularly American preference for seeing similarities and downgrading differences between cultures, and the risk of anachronistic interpretation is very high.

An equally reprehensible tendency is to avoid the challenge of determining exactly what these ancient people were talking about but moving quickly to a generalized correspondence in the modern world. In this thinking, surely AIDS (or skin color, or some similar physical or psychological condition) *must* be the equivalent of that leprosy. Such an erroneous judgment fails to respect each society, ancient and modern, with its distinctive beliefs, values, and behaviors. To this end, the model of the healthcare system presented in this book is extremely valuable, since it is the system and society or culture that shapes the meaning and interpretation human beings give to their experiences.

The definitions and models presented in this book and applied to information in the four Gospels about sick people, their sicknesses, healers, and remedies can contribute to a richer and more precise understanding of these questions in antiquity. Armed with these insights, modern readers will be in a better position to draw truly respectful and relevant conclusions for their situations. That, at least, has been the author's experience not only in academia but also in seminars and workshops outside that setting, including pastoral care, over the past twenty-five years.

Tres Riches Heures du Duc de Berry:
The Canaanite woman implores Jesus to heal her daughter
Colombe, Jean (fl. 1467–1529)
Musée Condé, Chantilly, France.

DISCUSSION QUESTIONS

CHAPTER 1

1. Reflect on the primary value orientations of mainstream U.S. culture, or your own culture if it is different. By primary I mean the first choice, the dominant value. Does your experience confirm or question this cluster of values?

2. Recall the definitions of *healing* and *curing* from the perspective of medical anthropology. How are these terms used in your Bible? How do people use these terms in discussion? Would it be helpful to adopt these definitions and strive to use them more accurately?

3. On the basis of the medical anthropological definitions of these terms: Did Jesus ever cure anybody? Did anyone ever cure anybody in antiquity?

4. Definitions of a miracle include "an extraordinary phenomenon that is inexplicable in terms of familiar, everyday causation," and "something that contradicts the laws of nature." How do these or other definitions relate to the options that different cultures select: controlling or being subject to or living in harmony with nature in the Kluckhohn-Strodtbeck model? If nature was considered capricious, what kind of laws might it have? If the biblical world knew that nature was capricious and anyone anyone's control, how could it perceive that Jesus' benevolent activities were somehow contrary to the laws of nature?

CHAPTER 2

1. What occasioned medical anthropology to emerge as a sub-discipline of anthropology? If you have traveled or lived abroad, can you recall experi-

ences that highlighted differences between your culture and the one you were visiting? If you regularly rub shoulders with people of other cultures, what cultural differences have you noticed? If you have begun to read the Bible with culturally sensitive eyes, what distinguishing elements have you identified?

2. Discuss the following terms as understood in medical anthropology: health, sickness, disease, illness, curing, healing. What adjustments to your thinking do the new definitions require? Why are these adjustments important?

3. Using the healthcare system model, identify and discuss the three sectors (professional, popular, and folk) as you have experienced them in the United States (or a country more familiar to you). How would you classify and understand a medicine woman in the Native American tradition? Or *curanderas* (traditional women healers) in Hispanic cultures such as northern New Mexico, New York's Spanish Harlem, Texas, and elsewhere?

4. Apply Kleinman's model of the interaction with a healer (p. 31) to some healing reports in any Gospel. How does it help or hinder your understanding of Jesus' activity?

5. How do you understand the statement: Healing boils down to meaning and the transformation of experience (p. 35)? Within the context of efficacy (Does it work?), what does this mean to you? Does it help to interpret any of the healing stories in the New Testament (for example, Mark 1:40-45; Mark 7:31-37)?

CHAPTER 3

1. A model is a simplified way of explaining a complex reality. How do the two models presented in chapter 3 help to explain the complex reality of leprosy in the Bible, whether in the Old or New Testament?

2. In parts of India, no word or phrase exists for "Thank you." If you receive a gift, it is thought that the giver owes it to you. So why say thank you? Read Luke 17 carefully. What does the person actually intend by saying "Thank you" to Jesus (v. 17)? Does Jesus respond to this "thank you," or does he talk about something entirely different? What can a reader conclude from this Gospel story? Is there any insight or lesson that can be applied or transferred to the United States or any other culture? If so, how does that take place?

CHAPTER 4

1. It is always advisable to read a book of the Bible, such as Mark, at one sitting. If you have the time, do this and pay attention to the healing reports. Make a record of what you observe. Does the model in chapter 4 help you to identify and sort out the information you discover?

2. Commenting on cultural healing, physician Stirling Puck wrote: "So certainly my prejudice is all in favor of Western medicine. But, in fact, I believe that whatever works should be done, and there is so much of medicine that is not understood on a scientific basis that I am certainly not willing to say that Western medicine is all there is." How would you relate healing from a religious perspective with scientific Western medicine? If Western medicine so strongly reflects Western beliefs and values, how scientific (or objective) is it?

3. With regard to the professional sector, how do Mark and Luke differ concerning physicians? (cf. Mark 5:26//Luke 8:43). When they use the word *physician,* what are they really talking about? Does it relate at all to the modern concept of *physician?*

4. In the popular sector as reflected in Mark, how are the categories of individual, family, social network, and community beliefs and practices related? Can you build a bridge between any of those understandings and your own contemporary experience? Is this bridge structurally safe—that is, will it be adequate to the cross-cultural challenge of comparing disparate systems, beliefs, values, practices?

5. How does Mark present Jesus as healer? Which sector does Jesus work in? What other activity is his healing activity linked with? What would that mean to his clients?

CHAPTER 5

1. As with the Gospel of Mark, take the time to read the Gospel of Matthew in one sitting. Pay attention to the healing stories and make notes as you read. Why are so many accounts of mighty deeds clustered in chapters 8 and 9?

2. What did you know, or have you learned, about the evil eye (see Matt 20:15)? People of Italian, Hispanic, or Middle Eastern ancestry would be familiar with this idea, and so would others. Explore this notion among friends or neighbors whose ethnic background is different from yours.

3. References to the evil eye occur in the Old Testament in these in-

stances: Deut. 15:9; 28:54, 56; Prov. 23:6; 28:22; Sir. 14:3, 6, 8, 9, 10; 31:13; 37:11; Tobit 4:7, 16. In the New Testament, even Jesus refers to this reality more than once: Matt. 6:22-23; 20:1-15; Mark 7:22; Luke 11:34-36; Gal. 3:1, 4:14 (spit, rather than despise; spitting being a common strategy for deflecting the evil eye). The phrase *evil eye* rarely appears in the translations, but one should find similar words, such as grudge, envy, and the like. Usually behind these latter words, the Hebrew or Greek literally has evil eye. As you read these passages, draw up a scenario of how human well-being is affected by the evil eye.

4. Moonstruck is another folk problem that is distinctive in Matthew's Gospel. What "meaning in life" did Jesus restore to moonstruck people (Matt. 3:24; 17:15)? Particularly in the latter report, what did Jesus remedy? Why were Jesus' disciples, whom he empowered to heal (Matt. 10:1), unsuccessful? What might you conclude about these folk healers?

CHAPTER 6

1. In identifying himself as physician in a figurative sense (4:23), Jesus also adds that he is a prophet who exorcises and heals (4:24). Prophets in the Bible were specialists in announcing the will of God for the here-and-now. How would such a prophetic function relate to healing? Might this have some relevance to the contemporary world?

2. The spirit holds a central place in Luke–Acts. He reports spirit-related illnesses, but also notes other interventions by spirits in human life and experience. Spirit is not so central a concept in Western cultures. However, Jesus' success against spirits in his world clearly carries political significance. Does this concept translate to the modern world? How might it be done by healthcare professionals, or by pastoral ministers?

3. Review the characteristics common to folk healers across cultures (pp. 101–2). In recent years, congregation-based healthcare opportunities (often headed by a nurse) have become very popular. What might people involved in such ventures incorporate from the characteristics of folk healers?

4. Modern believers are accustomed to thinking about human beings in terms of body and soul. These concepts are foreign to the Bible; they emerged in post-biblical Christianity under the influence of Greek philosophy. The Bible rather understands human beings in terms of three symbolic body-zones. How does this new way of reading biblical statements about human beings change your perspective? What insight does it offer about Jesus' healing intentions and activity?

5. In seminars on healing in the Bible, participants seem to focus on blindness as a physical deficiency, and wonder how Jesus might have remedied the physical problem. If the biblical report actually appears to contrast refusal to understand with insight and willingness to understand Jesus, what might healthcare professionals or pastoral ministers learn from this to incorporate in their repertoire?

CHAPTER 7

1. Contemporary Christians are fond of saying that Jesus and Christianity are counter-cultural. It is more accurate to say that they are actually counter-structural. This means they disagree with, and contest against, prevailing social structures. Healthcare delivery in the modern Western world is superb, yet in so many ways it leaves much to be desired. People critical of it do not want to destroy it but reform it. They can think of ways to improve the structure of healthcare. Taking as an example either a religiously sponsored institution (for example, a nursing home or a hospital) or a specifically structured service (for example, an HMO; PPO; etc.), what structural changes would seem to be desirable to make it conform closer to the healing activity of Jesus?

2. If John's is truly an anti-society, then indeed it is in conflict with the prevailing society. It is less interested in reforming that society and more interested in carving out a safe niche for itself. From such a scenario, are there any lessons or values that can be drawn into the contemporary world?

3. How might the understanding of sin as breach of interpersonal relations (less with God than with others) affect the healing activities of people in pastoral ministry? For example, in a large Roman Catholic diocese a priest suspected of and charged with sexually molesting children was eventually permitted to return to ministry in that congregation. Not only did he not apologize but he refused to clear up residual doubts. Instead he berated the congregation in his first sermon. How would you evaluate the priest's interpersonal relations with the community in this instance? Who was healed or not healed? What more might the healers do? What ought the candidate for healing do?

4. What irony do you notice in the healing of the man at the pool? A person with no one to help him, who is dislodged from society in general, is healed by Jesus. Then to cement his newly regained position in the larger society, he reports to and ingratiates himself with the opponents of Jesus, the person who helped him. Was the healed man an ingrate? Was he just doing

his duty? Can you think of analogous experiences in contemporary faith communities?

5. Again we return to consider the healing of the blind person. How does the concept of cultural healing assist in understanding John's report about Jesus? What relevance might that have for contemporary healthcare ministry?

GLOSSARY

AMERICANS IN GENERAL have been trained to consult Webster's (or any) dictionary when they don't know what a word means or when they want to define a term or concept in an essay they are writing. Americans will quote from the English dictionary to help clarify their position. When writing a term paper on healing in the Bible, students frequently quote Webster's definition of disease. The problem with such a definition should be obvious to the reader of this book. Americans read the Bible in English translation and are at the mercy of a translator. Does the ancient Hebrew or Greek language have a word that means "disease" in the same way that modern Western readers understand it? Did the English translator's culture influence her or his choice of English words? The English dictionary, therefore, is best for helping with correct spelling and the etymology of English words. Its definitions, however, reflect Western culture and are not helpful for understanding and interpreting the Bible.

Sophisticated readers interested in ancient healing practices might consider consulting a contemporary medical dictionary. Once again, "Webster" or someone similar comes to the rescue. When my wife was ill with ovarian cancer, we purchased *Merriam Webster's Medical Desk Dictionary* (henceforth MDD; Springfield, Mass.: Merriam-Webster Inc., 1993), a relatively inexpensive and comprehensive reference for medical terms and meanings based on actual contemporary usage. While it was a very helpful resource for our experience with the medical world specializing in cancer, it is less useful (perhaps entirely useless) for trying to understand healing in the ancient world.

This glossary collects some key terms that are used throughout this book. The meanings are drawn chiefly from the anthropological disciplines (medical, psychological, Mediterranean, etc.). These meanings are very likely not familiar to modern readers. The challenge will be to set aside our

151

modern medical understanding in order to appreciate the concepts and terms used by a culture that existed long before the invention of the microscope. Where it is appropriate in this glossary, I contrast the modern medical meanings with the meanings drawn from medical anthropology. Because understanding the Bible demands cross-cultural understanding and interpretation, only the anthropological disciplines can help meet this challenge adequately. Anything less will result in an ethnocentric interpretation and will skew the interpretation of the Biblical text beyond recognition.

aetiological—(British) see etiology.

contagion—the transmission of a reality, e.g., a disease, by direct or indirect contact. A contagious disease is an infectious disease that is communicated by contact with someone who has the disease, or with a bodily discharge of such a person, or with an object touched by such a patient or the patient's bodily discharges (MDD). So-called leprosy in the Bible was not a disease. The reality that was transmitted by touch was not a disease but rather dirt. People who had this problem were considered unclean. Touching someone unclean or sitting on something unclean rendered that person unclean, even though he or she did not contract the skin problem. Hence the fear was of pollution rather than contagion.

culture-bound syndrome—A syndrome is a group of signs and symptoms that occur together and characterize a particular health abnormality. A culture-bound syndrome is an abnormality that is distinctive in a culture because that cluster of signs and symptoms is given an interpretation that is usually not biomedical but rather social or cultural. Culture-bound syndromes are those folk-conceptualized disorders, that is, illnesses that include alterations of behavior and of experiences among their symptomology. The effects of being the object against whom someone has cast an evil eye form a culture-bound syndrome in circum-Mediterranean cultures. Western observers often identify no disease in such a person, but the person's behavior and experiences are indeed altered. Sometimes this healthy person dies, suddenly, because of cultural beliefs concerning the evil eye. Anthropologists use the term *culture-bound syndrome* with caution because it appears to mask ethnocentrism. Anything that does not fit into Western categories or perceptions is often labeled as culture-bound.

curing—Medical dictionaries (e.g. MDD) tend to view curing and healing as synonyms. In this perspective, both words mean to restore to health, soundness or normalcy. Medical anthropology distinguishes curing from healing. Curing is the strategy of destroying or checking a pathogen, removing a malfunctioning or non-functioning organ, restoring a person to health or well-being. It occurs rarely.

disease—is not a reality; it is an explanatory concept of the reality, sickness. From a biomedical perspective, this word describes an impairment of the normal state of the living animal or plant body or any of its components that interrupts or modifies the performance of the vital functions. It is a response to environmental factors (e.g., climate, malnutrition, industrial hazards), to specific infective agents (e.g., viruses, bacteria, worms), or to a combination of these factors. Medical dictionaries consider disease, sickness, and illness to be synonyms for a reality. Medical anthropology distinguishes these explanatory concepts and accepts the given definition for disease as a perspective on the reality 'sickness'.

doctor—In the contemporary world, a person who has earned one of the highest academic degrees conferred by a University, e.g., a Ph.D. A secondary meaning is one specializing in the healing arts, particularly a physician, surgeon, dentist, or veterinarian licensed to practice his or her profession.

efficacy—the ability of a healer or a material to produce a decided decisive, claimed, or desired result or effect. Actually, efficacy is a construct of a medical system and therefore a cultural construct. People are socialized into a particular understanding of healing that contains a socially legitimated model of effective healing. Modern medical science tends to consider efficacy as a matter of quantifying empirical effects. The successful results of placebos and non-specific psychosomatic therapies raise significant doubts about the value of relying exclusively on empirical effects.

emic—Kenneth L. Pike <www.sil.org/klp/eticemic.htm> originally employed the terms etic and emic. Generally speaking, emic is the native view, the perspective from within any system under study, the insiders' views. The emic view includes the shared ideology and perceptions of phenomena by members of a given society. Thus, natives in Matthew's community apparently recognized an illness that they called moonstruck (Matt 4:24; 17:15). This is the emic perspective. English translators routinely render this as 'epileptic', representing the translator's etic perspective (q.v.). Both perspectives are an integral part of the discipline of cross-cultural studies.

ethnomedicine—"The study of how members of different cultures think about disease and organize themselves toward medical treatment and the social organization of the treatment itself" (Fabrega cited in Johnson and Sargent 1990: 127); or more broadly, "the vast body of knowledge which has resulted from the curiosity of anthropologists about the medical beliefs and practices of members of traditional societies" (Foster and Anderson cited in Johnson and Sargent 1990: 127). Most often, ethnomedicine focuses on non-Western medical systems and the study of their beliefs and practices.

etic—a view from outside a system under study. An outsider observer's viewpoint of a society's ideology or phenomena. Modern Western readers of ancient Mediterranean texts like the Bible often begin by imposing their Western perspective on this ancient Mediterranean text as a first step in interpretation. If the process stops here, the interpretation will be ethnocentric. If the process continues, this imposed etic (outsider) perspective can gradually evolve to a derived etic perspective, that is one that reflects the ancient understanding fairly and accurately in modern categories from an entirely different culture. (See J. J. Pilch, "Altered States of Consciousness: A 'Kitbashed' model," *Biblical Theology Bulletin* 26 [1996] 133–38).

etiology—all the causes of a disease or abnormal condition. Etiological treatment seeks to remove or correct the causes of a disease. Etiology is also the branch of medical science that deals with the causes and origins of diseases. Modern medical perspectives focus on a single, naturalistic cause, often within or attributable to the person. In non-Western cultures (and sometimes within Western culture, too), the focus will be on a personal cause asking who (who is responsible for this: spirit? a demon? God?), what, and why. Often the patient is not responsible. This latter perspective is evident in the discussion centered on the healing of the man born blind in John 9. (See Foster 1976.)

explanatory model (EM)—a more or less formally structured and coherent account of reality. In truth, these models are frequently ambiguous, contradictory, and reflect various degrees of logical development. In human health and sickness considerations, the explanatory model is a set of beliefs about any or all of five issues: etiology; onset of symptoms, pathophysiology; course of the sickness (that is, severity and type of sick role); and treatment. Explanatory models are peculiar to individuals rather than cultures, and they change over the duration of the sickness. Professionals use an EM that differs from a lay EM, or a family EM, and so on. In the West, every patient experiences differences in EMs when trying to explain to a physician what the health problem is. The patients gropes for words while the physician is stymied because the patient is not using the technical vocabulary familiar to the physician EM. Nevertheless, the fact is that most people have multiple belief systems to which they turn when in need of help.

folk—this is an ambiguous and sometimes embarrassing word in anthropology. 'Primitive,' 'peasant,' and 'folk' were eventually replaced by 'rural' and 'agrarian,' or something similar. In the context of the three sectors of health care discussed in this book (professional, popular, and folk), the word *folk* refers to the non-professional, non-bureaucratic, specialist sector of a society that combines many different components. Some folk elements derive from the professional section, but most are related to the popular sector. Thus an individual is a patient in the professional sector, a client in the popular sector, and a sick family member in the folk sector. The model was proposed by Kleinman (1980) and adopted by other medical anthropologists as well.

folk-medicine—"traditional medicine as practiced non-professionally by people isolated from modern medical services, and involving especially the use of vegetable remedies on an empirical basis" (thus WDD). Folk medicine differs from primitive medicine in that it is nested in a pocket culture within a larger context. Traditions of the politically dominant culture have seeped into folk medicine over historical time. Folk culture therefore is a more open system of beliefs and behaviors than societies we call primitive, which are characterized by transmission of beliefs and behaviors in a closed system lacking the opportunities found in a situation of culture contact (see Romanucci-Ross 1969).

folk-conceptualized disorder—this phrase is an attempt to avoid the ethnocentric overtones of *culture-bound syndrome*. Both describe the same reality.

healer/heal/healing—in medical anthropology, healing is the restoration of meaning to life. It is the strategy of restoring social and personal meaning for life problems that accompany human health misfortunes. An etic expression of this idea is: healing is a process by which disease and certain worrisome circumstances are made into illness (which is a cultural construction and therefore meaningful) and give some degree of satisfaction through the reduction, or even the elimination of the psychological, sensory, and experiential oppressiveness engendered by a person's medical circumstances. Healing takes place always, infallibly, *if* the patient wants it. And perhaps for some, the rejection of meanings available for the experience of misfortune is itself a discovery of meaning. "My situation is hopeless; this healer won't (or no healer can) help me; I wish I would die." In the ancient world, those who did not trust that Jesus could help them did not experience the healing he could mediate. "And he could do no mighty work there, except that he laid his hands upon a few sick people and healed them. And he marveled because of their lack of loyalty" (Mark 6:5-6).

health—the condition of an organism or one of its parts in which it performs its vital function normally or properly: the state of being sound in body or mind, especially freedom from physical disease and pain (MDD). Actually, health is difficult to define, and it varies from culture to culture. The definition offered clearly reflects Western values and the emphasis on doing, action, achievement: a person's ability to function usefully in society. Blindness in antiquity wasn't understood as lack of an ability to perform a vital function. Blind people emanated darkness from within their bodies, as sighted people emanated light. Both could function in that society within their abilities.

illness—not a reality, but an explanatory concept of the reality 'sickness', which focuses on the social and cultural dimensions of a human health misfortune. It is the social and personal perception of socially disvalued states including but not necessarily restricted to what modern Western science would identify as a disease. In the Bible, to be moonstruck (Ps. 121:6; Matt. 4:24; 17:15) is an example of an illness.

leprosy—"a chronic disease caused by infection with an acid-fast bacillus of the genus *Mycobacterium (M. Leprae)* and characterized by the formation of nodules on the surface of the body and especially on the face or by the appearance of tuberculoid macules on the skin that enlarge and spread and are accompanied by loss of sensation followed sooner or later in both types if not treated by involvement of nerves with eventual paralysis, wasting of muscle and production of deformities and mutilations" (MDD). There is no evidence that this disease occurs anywhere on the pages of the Bible. The disease itself is minimally contagious and takes approximately ten years to incubate from time of infection.

meaning—meaning derives from the social system, not from the dictionary. To understand the meaning that people and/or their culture attribute to a sickness experience, one must know that culture's social system. Thus, the Israelite concern with purity ("You shall be holy as the Lord your God is holy"; see Lev. 11:45) is a key element of its social system. Flaws on the human body, like skin lesions (called leprosy in the Bible), render that person impure or unclean and not holy. While modern, Western, scientifically oriented readers think of germs and contagion in these instances (one meaning dictated by their social system), the ancient person experiencing this affliction and those witnessing it would think in terms of pollution. A person who came in contact with a polluted person might never display the same symptoms, but that contact is automatically polluting and renders that person impure, unclean, and not holy.

The difficulty yet necessity of keeping an interpreter's cultural bias out of the interpretation of an event under investigation leads anthropologists to distinguish between the etic perspective (the outsider's interpretation) and the emic perspective (the native view). Yet even this distinction can be deceptive since meanings are not always so well defined, and meanings may not be held in common by all members of a given culture.

medical anthropology—sometimes called ethnomedicine, this is the comparative study of medical systems in two or more cultures. In particular, it is "a conceptual system centered on the social and experiential particularities of sickness and healing" (Young 1982).

medicocentrism—a term patterned after ethnocentrism. It describes the view that modern, scientific Western medicine is the measure by which all sicknesses of all times and cultures ought to be evaluated.

nocebo—opposite of placebo; an inert or intrinsically innocuous item that can and does cause real damage. In some forms of witchcraft, sticking pins in a doll or an image of a person one wants to harm can indeed cause harm if both people share that belief system.

physician—a doctor of medicine. In antiquity, this word carried a very different meaning from the one we are accustomed to give it. In fact, there is no equivalent in antiquity to the modern physician or doctor of medicine.

placebo—an inert or intrinsically innocuous item prescribed more for the mental relief of the patient than for its actual effect on the disorder. The item is effective because of the patient's belief system. A common dictum in modern medicine is: all healing is faith healing. If one believes in it, that item can be effective according to one's belief system. And all persons have multiple belief systems that they use in times of need (e.g., medicine; prayer; pilgrimage; folk remedies; etc.).

pollution—a condition of physical impurity or uncleanness.

popular—One of the three sectors of the healthcare system. It includes the family and community, and embraces the lay, non-professional, non-specialist popular culture. It is the largest part of any system, and its major interest is health and health maintenance, not sickness and cure. At the same time, this is the arena in which the misfortune is first labeled and defined within several levels: individual, family, social network, and community beliefs.

primitive—a term in anthropology that describes a culture lacking a written language; also a culture characterized by low-level technology, small numbers, few contacts outside its own society, and homogeneity. Sometimes this culture is described as pre-literate or non-literate. See the observation above in *folk* (on the ambiguity of these terms, see Foster 1976).

professional—in modern times, a special status in the division of labor supported by official and sometimes public belief that it is worthy of such status (Freidson 1970: 187). We speak of the physician as a professional and consider education and licensing. But we also speak of athletes as professionals, yet this has little connection with education, special training, or licensing. In antiquity, there was no official acknowledgment of special status for the physician, and public belief in this status varied (see Horstmanshoff 1990). In the Bible, Sirach 38:1-15 reflects this ambiguity about the physician's status. In Mediterranean culture, status like honor can be ascribed (sex or gender; age; birth; etc.) or achieved (marriage; occupation; cf. Sir. 38:24–39:11; see Pilch, John J. 1991d. *Introducing the Cultural Context of the Old Testament*. New York/Mahwah: Paulist Press, p. 126).

purity—is an abstract way of interpreting data and is best understood in terms of its opposite: dirt. Whatever is out of place and violates a classification system is dirt. The grass-cutter whose shoes bring grass clippings into the home has brought dirt into the home. Grass belongs outdoors not indoors. Indoors, grass makes the home dirty. Purity is a way of ordering and classifying things, persons, places, activities and times. Ordering and classifying usually entails drawing lines and making boundaries. Purity rules therefore provide a map or series of maps that diagram a group's cultural system and locate "the proper place for everything and everything in its proper place." The holy (pure) community of God allowed only whole persons to be members. "He whose testicles are crushed or who male member is cut off shall not enter the assembly of the Lord. No bastard shall enter the assembly of the Lord; etc." (Deut. 23:1-2).

semantic illness network—the cluster of interrelated words, situations, symptoms, and feelings that a sufferer associates with an illness and that give the experience meaning for the sufferer. Semantic illness networks are the products of EMs.

sickness—in medical anthropology, this is the reality. This is the misfortune or irregularity in well-being that people recognize. This reality can be viewed from two perspectives and described by one of two explanatory concepts: disease and illness.

therapist—in general and in modern medicine, a person trained in methods of treatment and rehabilitation other than the use of drugs or surgery (e.g., occupational therapist, psychotherapist, and the like). In this book, we adopt a broader understanding: anyone who is recognized as capable of helping in health misfortune.

therapy—a treatment designed or serving to bring about rehabilitation or social adjustment.

value orientation—or value preferences. A value is an emotionally anchored commitment to pursue and support certain directions in life or types of action in life. A value orientation or value preference is any society's determination to esteem one choice more than another. The Mediterranean value orientation in human activity is spontaneity (being) while the Western value orientation or preference in human activity is planned and calculated activity (doing, achievement). Sickness is evaluated differently according to a culture's dominant value orientation (e.g., spontaneity versus achievement). See Pilch and Malina 1993: xv–xl "Introduction."

GENERAL BIBLIOGRAPHY

Abu-Lughod, Lila. 1986. *Veiled Sentiments: Honor and Poetry in a Bedouin Society*. Berkeley: Univ. of California Press.

Alexander, Linda. 1982. "Illness Maintenance and the New American Sick Role." Pp. 351–67 in Chrisman and Maretzki.

Anderson, Johs. G. 1980. "Leprosy in Translations of the Bible." *The Bible Translator* 31 (1980) 207–12.

Avalos, Hector. 1999. *Health Care and the Rise of Christianity*. Peabody, Mass.: Hendrickson.

Berkman, Lisa F. 1981. "Physical Health and the Social Environment: A Social Epidemiological Perspective." Pp. 51–74 in Eisenberg and Kleinman.

Berry, John W., Ype H. Poortinga, Marshall H. Segall, and Pierre R. Dasen. 1992. *Cross-Cultural Psychology: Research and Applications*. Cross-Cultural Research and Methodology Series, 10. Newbury Park, Calif.: Sage.

Bleich, J. David. 1981. *Judaism and Healing: Halakhic Perspectives*. New York: Ktav.

Briggs-Meyers, Isabel, with Peter B. Meyers. 1980. *Gifts Differing*. 2d ed. Palo Alto, Calif.: Consulting Psychologists Press.

Callahan, Daniel. 1973. "The WHO Definition." *Hastings Center Studies* 1:77–87.

Caplan, Arthur L., H. Tristram Engelhardt Jr., and James J. McCartney, eds. 1981. *Concepts of Health and Disease: Interdisciplinary Perspective*. Reading: Mass.: Addison-Wesley.

Carlston, Charles E. 1980. "Proverbs, Maxims, and the Historical Jesus." *Journal of Biblical Literature* 99:87–105.

Cassell, E. J. 1976. "Illness and Disease." *Hastings Center Report* 6:27-37.

Chrisman, Noel J. and T. W. Maretzki, eds. 1982. *Clinically Applied Anthropology: Anthropologists in Health Science Settings*. Culture, Illness, and Healing 5. Dordrecht: D. Reidel.

Csordas, Thomas J. and Arthur Kleinman. 1990. "The Therapeutic Process." Pp. 1–25 in Johnson and Sargent.

Douglas, Mary. 1966. *Purity and Danger*. New York: Praeger.

————. 1970. "The Healing Rite." *Man* 5:302–8.

Dow, James. 1986. "Universal Aspects of Symbolic Healing: A Theoretical Synthesis." *American Anthropologist* 88:56-69.

Draguns, J. and Harry Triandis, eds. 1980. *Handbook of Cross-Cultural Psychology*. Vol. 6: *Psychopathology*. New Jersey: Allyn and Bacon.

Dupont, Louis. 1980. *Homo Hierarchicus: The Caste System and Its Implications*. Rev. ed. Trans. M. Sainsbury et al. Chicago: Univ. of Chicago Press. [French ed. 1966].

Eickelman, Dale F. 1989. *The Middle East: An Anthropological Approach*. 2d ed. Englewood Cliffs, N.J.: Prentice Hall.

Eilberg-Schwartz, Howard. 1990. *The Savage in Judaism: An Anthropology of Israelite Religion and Ancient Judaism*. Bloomington: Indiana Univ. Press.

Eisenberg, Leon. 1977. "Disease and Illness: Distinctions between Professional and Popular Ideas of Sickness." *Culture, Medicine and Psychiatry* 1:9–23.

Eisenberg, Leon, and Arthur Kleinman, eds. 1981. *The Relevance of Social Science for Medicine*. Dordrecht: D. Reidel.

Elliott, John H. 1988. "The Fear of the Lear: The Evil Eye from the Bible fo Li'l Abner." *Forum* 4, 4:42–71.

————. 1992. "Matthew 20:1-15: A Parable of Invidious Comparison and Evil Eye Accusation." *Biblical Theology Bulletin* 22:166–78.

————. 1993. *What is Social-Scientific Criticism?* Guides to Biblical Scholarship. Minneapolis: Fortress Press.

————. 1994. "The Evil Eye and the Sermon on the Mount: Contours of a Pervasive Belief in Social Scientific Perspective." *Biblical Interpretation* 2:51-84.

Engelhardt, H. Tristram Jr. 1981. "The Concepts of Health and Disease." Pp. 30–35 in Caplan et al.

————. 1986. "The Social Meanings of Illness." *Second Opinion* 1:26–39.

Etkin, Nina L. 1988. "Cultural Constructions of Efficacy." Pp. 299–320 in van der Geest and Whyte.

Fabrega, Horacio. 1971. "The Study of Medical Problems in Preliterate Settings." *Yale Journal of Biology and Medicine* 43:385–407.

————. 1974. *Disease and Social Behavior: An Interdisciplinary Perspective*. Cambridge: MIT Press.

Feinstein, Alvan R. 1973. "An Analysis of Diagnostic Reasoning, Part I and II." *Yale Journal of Biology and Medicine* 46:212–32; 264–83.

Ferraro, Gary P. 1994. *The Cultural Dimension of International Business*. 2d ed. Englewood Cliffs, N.J.: Prentice Hall.

Fitzmyer, Joseph A. 1981. *The Gospel According to Luke (I–IX)*. Anchor Bible 28. Garden City, N.Y.: Doubleday.

————. 1985. *The Gospel According to Luke (X–XXIV)*. Anchor Bible 28A. Garden City, N.Y.: Doubleday.

Fitzpatrick, Ray. 1984. "Lay Concepts of Illness." Pp. 11–31 in Ray Fitzpatrick, John Hinton, Stanton Newman, Graham Scambler, and James Thompson, eds. *The Experience of Illness*. London: Tavistock.

Foster, George M. 1976. "Disease Etiologies in Non-Western Medical Systems." *American Anthropologist* 78:773–82.

Foster, George M., and Barbara Anderson. 1978. *Medical Anthropology*. New York: John Wiley.

Foucault, Michel. 1970. *The Order of Things*. New York: Vintage.

Frank, Jerome. 1974. *Persuasion and Healing: A Comparative Study of Psycho-therapy*. New York: Schocken.

Freidson, Eliot. 1970. *The Profession of Medicine: A Study of the Sociology of Applied Knowledge*. New York: Harper & Row.

Gaines, Atwood D. 1982. "Knowledge and Practice: Anthropological Ideas and Psychiatric Service." Pp. 243–73 in Chrisman and Maretzki.

Gaines, Atwood D., and P. Farmer. 1986. "Visible Saints: Social Cynosures and Dysphoria in the Mediterranean Tradition." *Culture, Medicine and Psychiatry* 10:295–330.

Geertz, Clifford. 1976. "'From the Native's Point of View': On the Nature of Anthropological Understanding." Pp. 221–37 in *Meaning and Anthropology*. Ed. Keith H. Basso and Henry A. Selby. Albuquerque: Univ. of New Mexico Press. Reprinted in C. Geertz, *Local Knowledge: Further Essays in Interpretive Anthropology*. New York: Basic Books, 1983.

Giblin, C. H. 1980. "Suggestion, Negative Response, and Positive Action in St. John's Portrayal of Jesus (2:1-11; 4:46-54; 7:2-14; 11:1-44)." *New Testament Studies* 26:197–211.

Gilmore, David D. 1982. "Anthropology of the Mediterranean Area." *Annual Review of Anthropology* 11:175–205.

Gilmore, David D., ed. 1987. *Honor and Shame and the Unity of the Mediter-ranean*. A special publication of the American Anthropological Association 22; Washington, D.C.: American Anthropological Association.

Glick, Leonard B. 1967. "Medicine as an Ethnographic Category: The Gimi of the New Guinea Highlands." *Ethnology* 6:31–56.

Good, Byron J. 1977. "The Heart of What's the Matter: The Semantics of Illness in Iran." *Culture, Medicine and Psychiatry* 1:25–28.

Good, Byron J., and Mary Jo DelVecchio Good. 1981. "The Meaning of Symp-toms: A Cultural Hermeneutic Model of Clinical Practice." Pp. 165–96 in Eisenberg and Kleinman.

Grmek, Mirko D. 1989. *Diseases in the Ancient Greek World*. Trans. by M. Muellner and L. Muellner. Baltimore: Johns Hopkins Univ. Press.

Hahn, Robert A., and Arthur M. Kleinman 1983. "Biomedical Practice and Anthropological Theory: Frameworks and Directions." *Annual Review of Anthropology* 12:305–33.

Hall, Edward T. 1983. *The Dance of Life*. New York: Doubleday.

Halliday, Michael A. K. 1976. "Anti-languages." *American Anthropologist* 78:570–84.

————. 1978. *Language as Social Semiotic: The Social Interpretation of Language and Meaning*. Baltimore: Univ. Park.

Hanson, K. C. 1993. "Blood and Purity in Leviticus and Revelation." *Listening:*

Journal of Religion and Culture 28:215–30.
<www.stolaf.edu/people/kchanson/blood.html>

Hanson, K. C. and Douglas E. Oakman. 1998. *Palestine in the Time of Jesus: Social Structures and Social Conflicts*. Minneapolis: Fortress Press.
<www.stolaf.edu/people/kchanson/ptj.html>

Harwood, Alan, ed. 1981. *Ethnicity and Medical Care*. Cambridge: Harvard Univ. Press.

Hemer, Colin J. 1986. "Medicine in the New Testament World." Pp. 43–83 in *Medicine and the Bible*. Bernard Palmer, ed. Exeter: Paternoster.

Henderson, George. 1989. *Understanding Indigenous and Foreign Cultures*. Springfield, Ill.: Charles C. Thomas.

Henderson, George, and Martha Primeaux. 1981. *Transcultural Health Care*. Menlo Park, Calif.: Addison-Wesley.

Herzfeld, Michael. 1986. "Closure as Cure: Tropes in the Exploration of Bodily and Social Disorder." *Current Anthropology* 27:107–20.

Hill, Carole E., ed. 1985. *Training Manual in Medical Anthropology*. Washington, D.C.: American Anthropological Association.

Hobbs, T. R. 1985. *2 Kings*. Word Biblical Commentary 13; Waco, Tex.: Word.

Hollenbach, Paul W. 1982. "Jesus, Demoniacs, and Public Authorities: A Socio-Historical Study." *Journal of the American Academy of Religion* 49:567–88.

Horstmanshoff, H. F. J. 1990. "The Ancient Physician: Craftsman or Scientist?" *Journal of the History of Medicine and Allied Sciences* 45:176–97.

Hughes, Charles C. 1968. "Ethnomedicine." In *International Encyclopedia of the Social Sciences*. New York: Free Press.

Hull, John M. 1974. *Hellenistic Magic and the Synoptic Tradition*. Naperville, Ill.: Alec R. Allenson.

Johnson, Thomas M., and Carolyn M. Sargent, eds. 1990. *Medical Anthropology: A Handbook of Theory and Method*. New York: Greenwood.

Kaplan, Marcie. 1983. "A Woman's View of DSM–III." *American Psychologist* July:786–803.

Kazmierski, Carl R. 1992. "Evangelist and Leper: A Socio-Cultural Study of Mark 1:40-45." *New Testament Studies* 38:37–50.

Kee, Howard Clark. 1983. *Miracle in the Early Christian World: A Study in Socio-historical Method*. New Haven: Yale Univ. Press.

———. 1986. *Medicine, Miracle, and Magic in New Testament Times*. SNTSMS 55. Cambridge: Cambridge Univ. Press.

Klein, Julie Thompson 1990. *Interdisciplinarity: History, Theory, and Practice*. Detroit, Mich.: Wayne State Univ. Press.

Kleinman, Arthur M. 1973. "Toward a Comparative Study of Medical Systems: An Integrated Approach to the Study of the Relationship of Medicine and Culture." *Science, Medicine, and Man* 1:55–65

———. 1974a. "Medicine's Symbolic Reality: On a Central Problem in the Philosophy of Medicine." *Inquiry* 16:206–13.

———. 1974b. "Cognitive Structures of Traditional Medical Systems: Ordering, Explaining, and Interpreting the Human Experience of Illness." *Ethnomedizin* III:27–49.

————. 1978. "Problems and Prospects in Comparative Cross-Cultural Medical and Psychiatric Studies." Pp. 407–40 in Kleinman et al., *Culture and Healing in Asian Societies.*

————. 1980. *Patients and Healers in the Context of Culture.* Berkeley: Univ. of California Press.

————. 1986. "Concepts and a Model for the Comparison of Medical Systems." Pp. 29–47 in Caroline Currer and Meg Stacey, eds. *Concepts of Health, Illness and Disease: A Comparative Perspective.* New York: Berg.

————. 1988. *Rethinking Psychiatry: From Cultural Category to Personal Experience.* New York and London: Free Press and Collier Macmillan.

Kleinman, Arthur M., Peter Kunstadter, E. Russell Alexander, and James L. Gate, eds. 1978. *Culture and Healing in Asian Societies: Anthropological, Psychiatric, and Public Health Studies.* Cambridge, Mass.: Schenkman.

Kleinman, Arthur M., and Lilias H. Sung. 1979. "Why Do Indigenous Practitioners Successfully Heal?" *Social Science & Medicine* 13B:7–26.

Kluckhohn, Florence R., and Fred L. Strodtbeck. 1961. *Variations in Value Orientations.* New York: Harper & Row.

Landy, David, ed. 1977. *Culture, Disease and Healing.* New York: Macmillan.

Lewellen, Ted C. 1983. *Political Anthropology: An Introduction.* South Hadley, Mass.: Bergin and Harvey.

Lewis, Gilbert. 1981. "Cultural Influences on Illness Behavior: A Medical Anthropological Approach." Pp. 151–62 in Eisenberg and Kleinman.

Lipowski. Z. 1969. "Psychosocial Aspects of Disease." *Annals of Internal Medicine* 71:1197–1206.

Logan, Michael H., and Edward E. Hunt Jr., eds. 1978. *Health and the Human Condition: Perspectives on Medical Anthropology.* North Scituate, Mass.: Duxbury.

Louw, Johannes P,. and Eugene A. Nida, eds. 1988. *Greek-English Lexicon of the New Testament Based on Semantic Domains.* 2 vols. New York: United Bible Societies.

Mackintosh, Douglas R. 1978. *Systems of Health Care.* Boulder, Colo.: Westview.

Malina, Bruce J. 1979. "The Individual and the Community—Personality in the Social World of Early Christianity." *Biblical Theology Bulletin* 9:126–38.

————. 1981. "The Apostle and Law: Prolegomena for an Hermeneutic." *Creighton Law Review* 14:1305–39.

————. 1983. "Why Interpret the Bible with the Social Sciences?" *American Baptist Quarterly* 2:119–33.

————. 1985. *The Gospel of John in Sociolinguistic Perspective.* Forty-eighth colloquy of the Center for Hermeneutical Studies, ed. Herman Waetjen. Berkeley: Center for Hermeneutical Studies. <www.stolaf.edu/people/kchanson/sociling.html>

————. 1986. *Christian Origins and Cultural Anthropology: Practical Models for Biblical Interpretation.* Atlanta: John Knox.

————. 1988. "Patron and Client: The Analogy Behind Synoptic Theology." *Forum* 4, 1:2–32. Reprinted in *The Social World of Jesus and the Gospels,* 143–75. London: Routledge, 1996.

————. 1989. "Christ and Time: Swiss or Mediterranean?" *Catholic Biblical Quarterly* 51 (1989):1–31

————. 1993. *The New Testament World: Insights from Cultural Anthropology.* Rev. ed. Louisville: Westminster John Knox.

————. 1994. "John's: The Maverick Christian Group: The Evidence of Sociolinguistics," *Biblical Theology Bulletin* 24:167–82. <www.stolaf.edu/people/kchanson/mav.html>

————. 1996a. "Reading Theory Perspectives." Pp. 3–31 in *The Social World of Jesus and the Gospels.* London: Routledge.

————.1996b. "Patron and Client: The Analogy behind Synoptic Theology." Pp. 143–75 in *The Social World of Jesus and the Gospels.* London: Routledge.

Malina, Bruce J., and Jerome H. Neyrey. 1988. *Calling Jesus Names: The Social Value of Labels in Matthew.* Sonoma, Calif.: Polebridge.

————. "Assessment of Gender and Sexual Contact in Israelite Societies: A Cross-Cultural Perspective," unpublished paper to be read in Chicago, October 1999.

Malina, Bruce J., and Richard L. Rohrbaugh. 1998. *Social-Science Commentary on the Gospel of John.* Minneapolis: Fortress Press. <www.lclark.edu/~rbaugh/john.html>

Mason, Randall C. Jr., Graham Clark, Robert R. Reeves Jr., and S. Bruce Wagner. 1969. "Acceptance and Healing." *Journal of Religion and Health* 8:123–42.

McElroy, Ann, and Patricia K. Townsend. 1989. *Medical Anthropology in Ecological Perspective.* 2d ed. Boulder: Westview [reprint of 1979].

McGoldrick, Monica, John K. Pearce, and Joseph Giordano, eds. 1982. *Ethnicity and Family Therapy.* New York: Guilford.

McKay, Heather A. 1992. "From Evidence to Edifice: Four Fallacies about the Sabbath." Pp. 179–99 in *Text as Pretext: Essays in Honour of Robert Davidson.* Robert P. Carroll, ed. JSOT Supplement Series 138. Sheffield: JSOT Press.

McKenney, James L., and Peter G. W. Keen. 1974. "How Managers' Minds Work." *Harvard Business Review* 52:79–90

Meier, John P. 1991. *A Marginal Jew: Rethinking the Historical Jesus.* Vol. 1: *The Roots of the Problem and the Person.* Anchor Bible Reference Library. New York: Doubleday.

————. 1994. *A Marginal Jew: Rethinking the Historical Jesus.* Vol. 2: *Mentor, Message, and Miracles.* Anchor Bible Reference Library. New York: Doubleday.

Mitchell, J. Clyde. 1969. "The Concept and Use of Social Networks." Pp. 1–50 in *Social Networks in Urban Situations.* J. Clyde Mitchell, ed. Manchester: Manchester Univ. Press.

Moerman, Daniel E. 1983. "Physiology and Symbols: The Anthropological Implications of the Placebo Effect." Pp. 156–67 in Romanucci-Ross et al.

Moerman, Daniel E. 1979. "Anthropology of Symbolic Healing." *Current Anthropology* 20:59–80.

Morley, Peter. 1978. "Culture and the Cognitive World of Traditional Medical Beliefs: Some Preliminary Considerations." Pp. 1–18 in Morley and Wallis.

Morley, Peter, and Roy Wallis, eds. 1978. *Culture and Curing: Anthropological*

Perspectives on Traditional Medical Beliefs and Practices. Pittsburgh: Univ. of Pittsburgh Press.

Murdock, George Peter. 1980. *Theories of Illness: A World Survey.* Pittsburgh: Univ. of Pittsburgh Press.

Neyrey, Jerome H. 1986a. "Body Language in 1 Corinthians: The Use of Anthropological Models for Understanding Paul and His Opponents." *Semeia* 35:129–70. Reprinted as: "Perceiving the Human Body: Body Language in 1 Corinthians." Pp. 102–46 in *Paul in Other Words: A Cultural Reading of His Letters.* Louisville: Westminster John Knox.

———. 1986b. "The Idea of Purity in Mark's Gospel," *Semeia* 35:91–128

———. 1994. "Despising the Shame of the Cross: Honor and Shame in the Johannine Passion Narrative," *Semeia* 69:113–37. <www.nd.edu./~jneyrey1/shame.html>

———. 1995. "Workbook for The Gospel of John: Theo 512." Unpublished class notes, Notre Dame Univ., Notre Dame, Ind.

Nissinen, Martti. *Homoeroticism in the Biblical World: A Historical Perspective.* Trans. K. Stjerna. Minneapolis: Fortress Press, 1998.

Noland, John. 1979. "Classical and Rabbinical Parallels to 'Physician, Heal Yourself' (Lk. IV 23)." *Novum Testamentum* 21:193–209.

Noorda, Sijbolt. 1979. "Illness and Sin, Forgiving and Healing." Pp. 215–24 in M. J. Vermaseren, ed. *Studies in Hellenistic Religions.* Etudes preliminaires aux religions orientales dans l'empire romain 78. Leiden: Brill.

Ohnuki-Tierney, Emiko. 1981. *Illness and Healing among the Sakhalin Ainu: Symbolic Interpretation.* Cambridge: Cambridge Univ. Press.

———. 1984. *Illness and Culture in Contemporary Japan: An Anthropological View.* Cambridge: Cambridge Univ. Press.

Palgi, Phyllis. 1983. "Mental Health, Traditional Beliefs, and the Moral Order among Yemenite Jews in Israel." Pp. 319–35 in Romanucci-Ross et al.

Palmer, Bernard, ed. 1986. *Medicine and the Bible.* Exeter, England: Paternoster.

Pamment, M. 1981. "Witch-hunt." *Theology* 84:98–106.

Papajohn, John, and John Spiegel. 1975. *Transactions in Families.* Jossey-Bass Behavioral Science Series. San Francisco: Jossey-Bass.

Pert, Candace B. 1997. *Molecules of Emotion: The Science behind Mind-Body Medicine.* New York: Simon and Schuster.

Pfifferling, John-Henry. 1981. "A Cultural Prescription for Medicocentrism." Pp. 197–222 in Eisenberg and Kleinman.

Pike, Kenneth L. 1969. "Language as Behavior and Etic and Emic Standpoints for the Description of Behavior." Pp. 114–31 in *Social Psychology: Reading and Perspective.* E. F. Borgatta, ed. Chicago: Rand-McNally.

Pilch, John J. 1981a. "Biblical Leprosy and Body Symbolism." *Biblical Theology Bulletin* 11:119–33.

———. 1981b. *Wellness: Your Invitation to Full Life.* San Francisco, Calif.: Harper and Row.

———. 1982. *Galatians and Romans.* Collegeville Bible Commentary 6; Collegeville, Minn.: Liturgical Press.

———. 1985a. "Healing in Mark: A Social Science Analysis." *Biblical Theology Bulletin* 15:142–50.

———. 1985b. *Wellness Spirituality.* New York: Crossroad.

———. 1986. "The Health Care System in Matthew: A Social Science Analysis." *Biblical Theology Bulletin* 16:102–6.

———. 1988a. "Interpreting Scripture: The Social Science Method." *The Bible Today* 26:13–19.

———. 1988b. "Understanding Biblical Healing: Selecting the Appropriate Model." *Biblical Theology Bulletin* 18:60–66.

———. 1988c. "Review of *Medicine and the Bible,* Bernard Palmer, ed." *Catholic Biblical Quarterly* 50:747–48.

———. 1988d. "Wellness Spirituality." *Health Values* 12:28–31.

———. 1989a. "Sickness and Healing in Luke–Acts." *The Bible Today* 27:21–28.

———. 1989b. "Reading Matthew Anthropologically: Healing in Cultural Perspective." *Listening: Journal of Religion and Culture* 24:278–89.

———. 1991a. "Sickness and Healing in Luke–Acts." Pp. 181–209 in *The Social World of Luke–Acts: Models for Interpretation.* Ed. Jerome H. Neyrey, S.J. Peabody, Mass.: Hendrickson.

———. 1991b. "Health in the New Testament: Did Healings Happen?" *National Outlook* (Australia) 13 (June):12–14.

———. 1991c. *Introducing the Cultural Context of the New Testament.* New York: Paulist.

———. 1992a. "Separating the Sheep from the Goats." *PACE (Professional Approaches for Christian Educators)* 21 (April):215–18.

———. 1992b. "A Spirit Named 'Fever.'" *PACE (Professional Approaches for Christian Educators)* 21 (May):253–56.

———. 1992c. "BTB Reader's Guide: Understanding Healing in the Social World of Early Christianity." *Biblical Theology Bulletin* 22:26–33.

———. 1993. "'Beat His Ribs While He Is Young' (Sir. 30:12): A Window on the Mediterranean World." *Biblical Theology Bulletin* 23:101–13.

———. 1994. "Secrecy in the Mediterranean World: An Anthropological Perspective." *Biblical Theology Bulletin* 24:151–57.

———. 1995. "Insights and Models for Understanding the Healing Activity of the Historical Jesus." *Hervormde Teologiese Studies* 51:314–37.

———. 1996a. "Altered States of Consciousness: A 'Kitbashed' Model." *Biblical Theology Bulletin* 26:133–38.

———. 1996b. "Healing." Pp. 413–20 in *The Collegeville Pastoral Dictionary of Biblical Theology.* Ed. Carroll Stuhlmueller. Collegeville, Minn.: Liturgical.

———. 1997. "BTB Reader's Guide: Psychological and Psychoanalytical Approaches to Interpreting the Bible in Social Scientific Context." *Biblical Theology Bulletin* 27:112–16.

———. 1998. "Appearances of the Risen Jesus in Cultural Context: Experiences of Alternate Reality." *Biblical Theology Bulletin* 28:52–60.

———. 1999. *The Cultural Dictionary of the Bible.* Collegeville, Minn.: Liturgical.

Pilch, John J., and Bruce J. Malina, eds. 1993. *Biblical Social Values and their Meaning*. Peabody, Mass.: Hendrickson. [2d ed.1998]

Pilisuk, Marc, and Susan Hillier Parks. 1986. *The Healing Web: Social Networks and Human Survival*. Hanover, N.H.: Univ. of New England Press.

Pontifical Biblical Commission. 1993. *The Interpretation of the Bible in the Church*. Rome: Libreria Editrice Vaticana.

Press, Irwin. 1982. "Witch Doctor's Legacy: Some Anthropological Implications for the Practice of Clinical Medicine." Pp. 179–88 in Chrisman and Maretzki.

Rhoads, David, Joanna Dewey, and Donald Michie. *Mark as Story: An Introduction to the Narrative of a Gospel*. 2d ed. Minneapolis: Fortress Press, 1999. <www.stolaf.edu/people/kchanson/markasstory.html>

Romanucci-Ross, Lola. 1969. "The Hierarchy of Resort in Curative Practices: the Admiralty Islands, Melanesia." *Journal of Health and Social Behavior,* 10:201–9.

———. 1978. "Melanesian Medicine: Beyond Culture to Method." Pp. 115–38 in Morley and Wallis.

Romanucci-Ross, Lola, Daniel E. Moerman, and Laurence R. Tancredi, eds. 1983. *The Anthropology of Medicine: From Culture to Method*. New York: Praeger.

Rosner, Fred. 1977. *Medicine in the Bible and the Talmud: Selections from Classical Jewish Sources*. New York: Ktav.

Ross, J. M. 1978. "Epileptic or Moonstruck?" *Bible Translator* 19:126–28.

Saler, Benson. 1977. "Supernatural as a Western Category." *Ethos* 5:21–33.

Saunders, Lyle. 1954. *Cultural Differences and Medical Care: The Case of Spanish Speaking People of the Southwest*. New York: Sage.

Saunders, Lyle, and Gordon Hewes. 1969. "Folk Medicine and Medical Practice." Pp. 402–08 in *The Cross-Cultural Approach to Health Behavior*. Ed. L. Riddick Lynch, Rutherford, N.J.: Farleigh Dickinson Univ. Press.

Scarborough, John. 1969. *Roman Medicine*. Ithaca, N.Y.: Cornell Univ. Press.

———. 1988. "Medicine." Pp. 1227–48 in *Civilization of the Ancient Mediterranean*. Michael Grant and Rachel Kitzinger, eds. New York: Charles Scribner's Sons.

Schultenover, David G. 1993. *A View from Rome: On the Eve of the Modernist Crisis*. New York: Fordham Univ. Press.

Schutz, Alfred. 1970. *Reflections on the Problem of Relevance*. Edited, annotated, and with an introduction by Richard M. Zaner. New Haven: Yale Univ. Press.

Seymour-Smith, Charlotte. 1986. "Medical Anthropology." in *Dictionary of Anthropology*. Boston: G.K. Hall & Co.

Sigerist, Henry E. 1961. *A History of Medicine*. New York: Oxford Univ. Press.

Simons, Ronald C., and Charles C. Hughes, eds. 1985. *The Culture-Bound Syndromes: Folk Illnesses of Psychiatric and Anthropological Interest*. Dordrecht: D. Reidel.

Spiegel, John. 1982. "An Ecological Model of Ethnic Families." Pp. 31–51 in McGoldrick et al.

Stewart, Edward C., and Milton J. Bennett. 1991. *American Cultural Patterns*. 2d ed. Yarmouth, Maine: Intercultural Press.

Theissen, Gerd. 1983. *Miracle Stories of the Early Christian Tradition*. Trans. F. McDonagh. Ed. J. Riches. Philadelphia: Fortress Press.

Turner, Bryan S. 1980. "The Body and Religion: Towards an Alliance of Medical Sociology and Sociology of Religion." *The Annual Review of the Social Sciences of Religion* 4:247–84.

Turner, Edith, with William Blodgett, Singleton Kahona, and Fideli Benwa. 1992. *Experiencing Ritual: A New Interpretation of African Healing*. Philadelphia: Univ. of Pennsylvania Press.

Twaddle, Andrew C. 1981. "Sickness and the Sickness Career: Some Implications." Pp. 111–33 in Eisenberg and Kleinman.

Unschuld, Paul U. 1976. "Western Medicine and Traditional Healing Systems: Competition, Cooperation or Integration?" *Ethics in Science & Medicine* 3:1–20.

————. 1980. "The Issue of Structured Coexistence of Scientific and Alternative Medical Systems: A Comparison of East and West German Legislation." *Social Science and Medicine* 14B:15–24.

————. 1988. "Culture and Pharmaceutics: Some Epistemological Observations on Pharmacological Systems in Ancient Europe and Medieval China." Pp. 179–97 in van der Geest and Whyte.

van der Geest, Sjaak. 1988. "Pharmaceutical Anthropology: Perspectives for Research and Application." Pp. 329–69 in van der Geest and Whyte.

van der Geest, Sjaak, and Susan Reynolds Whyte, eds. 1988. *The Context of Medicines in Developing Countries: Studies in Pharmaceutical Anthropology*. Dordrecht: Kluwer Academic.

van Hulse, E. 1975. "The Nature of Biblical 'Leprosy' and the Use of Alternative Medical Terms in Modern Translations of the Bible." *Palestine Exploration Quarterly* 107/2:87–105.

Veyne, Paul. 1988. "Rome: un société d'hommes." *L'histoire*. May, 1988: 76–78.

Weidman, Hazel Hitson. 1982. "Research Strategies, Structural Alterations and Clinically Applied Anthropology." Pp. 201–41 in Chrisman and Maretzki.

————. 1988. "A Transcultural Perspective on Health Behavior." Pp. 261–80 in David S. Gochman, ed. *Health Behavior: Emerging Research Perspectives*. New York: Plenum.

Wellin, Edward. 1978. "Theoretical Orientation in Medical Anthropology: Change and Continuity over the Past Half-Century." Pp. 23–51 in Logan and Hunt.

White, Hayden. 1973. "Foucault Decoded: Notes from Underground." *History and Theory* 12:23–54.

White, Leland J. 1986. "Grid and Group in Matthew's Community: The Righteousness/Honor Code in the Sermon on the Mount." *Semeia* 35:61–90.

Wilson, J. V. Kinnier. 1982. "Medicine in the Land and Times of the Old Testament." Pp. 337–65 in *Studies in the Period of David and Solomon*. Ed. Tomoo Ishida, Winona Lake, Ind.: Eisenbrauns.

Wink, Walter. 1984. *Naming the Powers: The Language of Power in the New Testament*. Vo. l: *The Powers*. Philadelphia: Fortress Press.

Worsley, Peter. 1982. "Non-Western Medical Systems." *Annual Review of Anthropology* 11:315–48.

Young, Allan. 1982. "The Anthropology of Illness and Sickness." *Annual Review of Anthropology* 11:257–85.

Zborowski, Mark. 1952. "Cultural Components in Responses to Pain." *Journal of Social Issues* 8:16–30.

————. 1969. *People in Pain.* Jossey-Bass Behavioral Science Series. San Francisco: Jossey-Bass.

Zola, Irving K. 1966. "Culture and Symptoms: An Analysis of Patients' Presenting Complaints." *American Sociological Review* 31:615–30.

A complete list of John J. Pilch's publications is available at: <www.stolaf.edu/people/kchanson/pilch.html>

SOME KEY JOURNALS

Medical Anthropology Quarterly—International Journal for the Cultural and Social Analysis of Health. Official journal of the *Society for Medical Anthropology* published by the American Anthropological Association.

Medical Anthropology Newsletter to 1984; then succeeded by *Medical Anthropology Quarterly* (above).

Medical Anthropology, Cross-Cultural Studies in Health and Illness. Published by Gordon and Breach Science Publishers.

Social Science and Medicine <www.elsevier.nl/inca/publications/store/3/1/5/>. Includes essays by anthropologists, sociologists, geographers, economists, and other social scientists.

Ethnomedizin (Hamburg, Germany)

Culture, Medicine and Psychiatry

Society for Ancient Medicine. <www.web1.ea.pvt.k12.pa.us/medant>

SCRIPTURE INDEX